THE ACCIDENTAL PSYCHIC

Acknowledgements

This book is dedicated to my husband, Norman – an extremely patient and kind man. I am more grateful than I can say to Sergio Repka for his help with putting the bits right that kept going wrong – a master proof-reader and adviser.

I would also like to thank Mike Allen, without whose great wisdom and insight this book would not have been completed.

The
ACCIDENTAL
PSYCHIC

A Handbook on Being Psychic

Mhairi Kent
with Margaret Paul

Cartoons by Bob Stokes

HARTLANDS PUBLICATIONS

First published in 2001 by
Hartlands Publications
PO Box 428
Isleworth
Middlesex
TW7 6WB
www.hartlands.co.uk

The right of Mhairi Kent to be identified as the author of this work
has been asserted by her in accordance with the Copyright,
Designs and Patents Act, 1988.

ISBN 0 9541069 0 3

Design and typesetting by Ex Libris Press
1 The Shambles, Bradford on Avon, Wiltshire

Printed in Britain by Cromwell Press, Trowbridge, Wiltshire

CONTENTS

Chapter 1

PREFACE

As I lay on my back with the largest amethyst I had ever seen placed strategically on my tummy, I wondered frantically what on earth I was doing in Rotterdam anyway, in the clinic of a world-renowned Holy Man. All my psychic vibes were lying in tattered ruins in the corner of the room, along with what remained of my ego – shot down in flames by this fiery and passionate 'enlightened one'. I thought of how strong I had believed my ability to be, and, if I'm honest, how special I was. I now saw myself as being lower than a worm and as gifted as a crêpe Suzette.

I stared fixedly at the cracked and flaking ceiling, as a series of people and events paraded themselves before my eyes – the forerunners and cause of my visit. I had visited this Holy Man in the hopes that he would immediately recognise how wonderful I was and in need of special and preferential care. This was of course not meant to be.

On my arrival at his clinic on the outskirts of Amsterdam I was shown into his treatment room: a stark white area with a couch, a chair and not much else. As I waited for him in the chair which had obviously done duty in a torture chamber, I was not particularly worried, just very tired after a rather difficult journey during which my credit cards and cash had been stolen.

He made an unobtrusive entrance behind me and then proceeded to sit cross-legged in front of me. He sat in silence – a quiet contained Indian with snowy hair and piercing eyes. I became aware of the flies buzzing round the room, and the murmur of voices elsewhere in the clinic; with a sorrowful sigh he stood up and crossed over to me. Passing his hands over my body at a distance of about 18 inches he grunted darkly and sat down again. "You are abnormal," he said at length. I was fairly sure I didn't want to be abnormal, just wonderful; but maybe it was all right.

"You have to learn to be normal, to go into the supermarket or shopping and no one will recognise that you are psychic. You are broadcasting on all frequencies – what a waste." I gave a guilty start – how on earth did he know that whenever I went to do my grocery shopping I was recognised for the wonderful being I was?

The week before I came to Amsterdam I had gone to get food for my husband to eat in my absence – whilst I was receiving training in being a wonderful and majestic psychic. Hardly had I crossed the threshold of the supermarket when a small intent woman came up to me. Looking up at me earnestly, she had complimented me (I think) on my enormous power. She said she had felt me coming into the shop and had to come to meet me. I would be less than human if I hadn't revelled in it on some level – me the superbeing. Much as I hate to admit it, the Holy Man was right – this is a very wasteful way with the precious energy of life. In fact this comment had been made to me by various people over the years but I certainly had 'not had ears' to hear it. If people can recognise that you are special then you are probably, like I was, abnormal. It's strange how things happen. Now I have come into my full power, I have to convince people I'm genuine, as they cannot pick that up from me any longer. Ah, me.

Although I had to accept the Holy Man's assessment of my 'psychicness', I disagreed profoundly with him about involvement in other people's lives. He gave me a long lecture about not taking on someone else's Karma. It was at this point that my rebellion began, and I realised that I would not now be sitting at his holy feet picking up gems of wisdom – or whatever it is you do at a Holy Man's feet. I passionately believed, and continue to believe, that the people that cross my path in trouble are there for me to help as much as I can. I am also aware on some deep level that I might have to return 25 times as a stag beetle to 'atone' for this, but I can't help it – I think I'm a born rescuer (or interferer!).

The Holy Man was not pleased that he could not persuade me to step back and leave things be: after my intervention in five knife fights, three road rages and two muggings over the last few years I'm still here, though I would not recommend that anyone tries to sort these difficult situations out. I suppose, to be candid, I am 'headstrong', or as my mother used to put it, as stubborn as an angry wasp.

I'm probably running out of guardian angels like other people run out of socks. In fact, in my accident-prone past, I have several times been granted a clear vision of exhausted angels sitting, head in hands, at a table. Their feet are resting in steaming bowls of water, and they are obviously due some extended leave of absence. I wonder how they fit into my Karma? Perhaps when I die there will be a line of angels all waiting to kick my butt!

The Holy man, looking at me as if I was indeed a rather nasty specimen of Stag Beetle, told me to lie down on the couch and look hard at my life.

"You have no power to speak of," he said as he left the room. "I will help you to take control of the little you have."

Not an auspicious start to my advancement in psychicness. My confidence drained out of my belly button as the amethyst did whatever it is that amethysts are meant to do.

To distract my skittering and unhappy thoughts, I obediently reviewed my life before my arrival in Amsterdam, and indeed my chequered career as 'mistress accident prone', or as the *Daily Mail* put it, 'The unluckiest lady in Britain'. This visit to Amsterdam was a most crucial turning point in my life, and despite my rather negative appraisal of what happened, I am profoundly grateful for being shown how to assess what my abilities are, how to develop them, and how to share this knowledge with others.

Chapter 2

CHILDHOOD ESCAPADES

I SUPPOSE THAT DURING MY accident-prone childhood, when I spoiled things and was generally rather disruptive towards my surroundings – whether animate or inanimate – I should have suspected the difference between me and my peers was the 'mind power' I would begin to learn of and control in later life. It is very surprising to me that this use of mental power is only now being accredited and used more effectively, especially as it made a significant contribution to the 'war effort'. My progress has been meteoric and painfully fast, in contrast to my parents' development.

My father, a tall Highland charmer, was the son of a Presbyterian minister and could transmit mind pictures across huge distances; my mother had the ability to receive and interpret these pictures. At various times during the war, my father was dropped by the RAF behind German lines and would make his way to the nearest airfield. He would then find somewhere to hide whilst he watched the arrival and departure of the planes. Just prior to his departure and before making his way to another airfield, he would transmit information about the number and type of planes and the location of the airfield to my mother.

They had agreed on a transmission time prior to his departure. My mother, discreet until her death bed, would never reveal the location of the control room to which she made her way. I often think of how bizarre the whole thing must have been to the people round her, as she solemnly read out the co-ordinates of the airfield, described the planes she could see and how many there were. I also remember my mum, in a rare moment of humour about the situation, said she had shocked the staff by mentioning as an aside that there was a large dog that seemed to ritually relieve itself on the planes prior to take off. I don't think they recorded that! In adulthood I have had many depressing encounters with telepathic assessment techniques – they have all failed to be alive, vibrant and exciting (or useful)!

My father was also one of the founder members of MENSA. He was one of the most humorous people I have ever met; handsome, charming and totally irresistible to women. This was in part due to his ability to project an image of himself that was not entirely true – he could cast illusions and glamours. I believe he inherited his many psychic abilities and 'knowings' from his gentle Highland mother, although she would never talk to him about it.

It was probably at an early age that my father received his first harsh lessons in learning to control and suppress the messages that poured into his brain from every side. Knowing things without being told was a serious sin in the church's eyes, unless it was 'the gift of prophecy', but, as grandfather said as he beat him with his belt, it was ungodly to know about forthcoming deaths. As he truly was a God-fearing man, it is likely that he beat my dad with reluctance, but because he thought it was for the good of my father's soul .

My father was also an acclaimed artist, painting realistic and beautiful scenes from his beloved Scotland; he was also an accomplished Scottish dancer and fisherman, and a respected aircraft designer. He designed two of the RAF's planes of the 1950's.

My mother, a tough upper middle class English woman, was a spiritual healer, working within the Church of England. Her mental psychic abilities were probably greater than my father's, and certainly wider: as well as receiving and interpreting any information transmitted by my father deliberately, she could, as already mentioned, provide extra information that he had not intentionally sent – they could supplement and augment each other's power. She could manipulate the outcome of races, draws, etc. and actually be a thoroughly naughty lady!

Mental psychic ability is exciting and encompasses all those mysterious and mystical terms we hear about in the press – telekinesis (the ability to move things without touching them), remote viewing, psychic surgery – they can give us delicious shudders down our spine – but I must stress that they are all abilities that can be accessed and controlled. We inherit our ease of access from our forebears, but whatever many of our modern-day gurus in this field may tell us, we all have the same psychic equipment to develop.

The Start of the Journey

It is hard to say when I became aware that I had inherited my parents' talents at least to some degree. I was born in a beautiful thatched cottage in Sussex, owned by my Godmother. My father was, as usual, working abroad on yet another secret mission and was not on the scene until I was three. He had continued as a 'spy' after the war. During this early period I was incredibly naughty and difficult towards my mother – I vividly remember dropping kittens from my bedroom window to see if they could fly. When I realised they couldn't, I helped them by using my mind to slow their descent – I think that this is something to do with time and that we can all do this without realizing it. How many times have you watched the kettle, hoping for a quick cup of coffee and it takes much longer than usual? In fact, there is even a humorous 'law' that states that this will happen.

I would probably not remember doing this if my mother had not imprinted the incident on my memory for ever. Fortunately the kittens were unhurt by the experiences, but my mother was gravely concerned. She sat next to me on the bed, her face very serious, and warned me that I was not to do this to the kittens; it was unfair to them. When I told her I could help them fly, she took both my hands and said I was never to do this again or I would have to go and live with someone else. Had she been angry with me I would have rebelled, but I felt her deep fear. She could – as I can – project very clear images to accompany her warning. How often do we warn our children to be careful, whilst (usually not deliberately) projecting to them pictures of what might happen if they are careless.

Shortly after this I clambered onto the shelf above a land drain – an open hole to take flood water from the fields. Once I was there, I was so frightened I couldn't remember how to block the hole again so that I could climb across. The emergency services looked for me for 24 hours, during which there was a flash flood that prevented them hearing me crying. When the rain abated they finally found me. The fireman who rescued me told my mother that he couldn't understand how I had got onto the shelf; they had to dig the ground away above me to get me out.

I mention throughout the book how incredibly eventful my life has always been: when I was three and a half my father returned to England and we joined him at the RAF station at Melksham where he was the commanding officer. He was highly disconcerted by my abilities, but also greatly amused. One day remains vividly in my memory. I was sitting in the garden playing in my sandpit, when I noticed a large snake lying in the shade of a bush. I crossed to the snake and started to stroke its head. Immediately it woke up, and within a few minutes it was lying in coils round me.

When my poor mother came to get me for lunch she was panic-stricken. She had just heard on the radio that a large boa constrictor had escaped from the local zoo, and that it was probably hungry. She did not know what on earth to do. This to my mind is the most frustrating part of usually being Mrs Powerhouse – if those you love are involved you are 'cut off' from your inner vision, and frankly, common sense! Finally, she went back into the house and called the police. They arrived with the zoo-keeper in a very short time indeed. The keeper came into the garden and suggested to me that the snake would probably like to sleep on its own and that it was hungry and would like its lunch. I climbed out of the coils, gently patting the snake on the head. I didn't see the keeper remove the snake, but I knew he wasn't hurting it because the snake would have told me. This was the first experience I had of mind pictures from an animal. I believe absolutely that all children have this ability and that we lose it as we mature.

I went to nursery school at four and did not enjoy it at all. I was a complete nightmare to the teachers as they could not keep me in the school. It is very easy indeed to fool oneself – let alone others – into thinking that you have locked the door when you haven't, or to think you have put the front door key in your pocket when it is still in the house. However I did it, I rapidly gained a reputation for being able to walk through locked doors. I know that many mystics in the East are reputed to be able to change matter and I have a feeling that in fact I could do this too – unfortunately I have now lost this ability!

On one fine summer's day, having once again made my escape, I was returning as usual through the wood that lay between the school and my home. The wood – long since built on – was a rather neglected ramble of half-grown trees, stunted by a lack of light from the huge trees that dominated the area. I loved the way the sun shone through the leaves and played on the plants that grew among the little bushes, especially the bluebells. The wood was full of birds and rustlings. I skipped happily along, enjoying my freedom, when I became aware that the birds had stopped singing, that a man had followed me into the wood and was striding after me. He told me to wait for him, he had something to show me. Feeling very frightened I hid in a bush. The man proceeded through the wood banging and prodding each tree and bush as he made his way towards me. When he reached my bush I 'made myself invisible'; he walked past it, still calling me, and cursing and swearing. I remained cowering in the bush until my father came to look for me. In direct comparison with my locked door exploits this is simple to explain; we recognise each other through the energy fields that surround us, and by suppressing these we effectively become invisible. This technique is discussed further in the book and is a tool readily accessible to all.

When I spoke to the police later (the man was a 'restricted inmate' from the local mental home) instinct even at that age warned me not to mention that I had become 'one with the bush'. I think this technique is what the Egyptians called shape-shifting. Afterwards, in a rare display of affection, my father congratulated me both for hiding so well and for being discreet.

My father then went to Korea and was officially missing, presumed dead, for five years. My life was again disrupted: my mother and I fell through a hole in the system – because Dad was on a secret mission, and they knew perfectly well that he was alive we could not receive his pension. The RAF froze his pay and in addition to having to leave the house at Melksham, there was no money to live on.

My mother took a job as a live-in cook at various boarding schools and was unable to keep me with her, so I attended my first boarding school at four and a half, returning to a foster home at the weekends. That was the pattern of my life for the next five years – I left the first foster home as the lady I was with found me 'creepy', I'm glad to say. She and her two strapping sons had various pets they took delight in tormenting. I took equal delight in helping all the mice and rabbits to escape to new homes by using my thoughts to undo the locks when no one was looking. The dog was more of a problem, but I showed him how to undo the fridge door and after multiple raids on the sausages and cream they found a new home for him..

On my last weekend at the foster home, I hardly got through the door when I was met by a harpy – talons outstretched to rend me limb from limb. It took me a moment or two to recognise the lady of the house. She shrieked at me like a banshee for ten minutes, all the while listing my misdemeanours.

"Don't look so innocent – even though you are only five you

are steeped in wickedness – we know you conjured demons to release our precious animals." I didn't listen any further, but waited for the tirade to finish. I wondered what on earth had brought this on – all that was old hat. I stopped contemplating the large spider that was hanging from a thread and was about to land on her head – I would no doubt get the blame for that too!

She had now reached the peak of her fury, and pointing a shaking finger at me told me that it was not amusing to kick a hornet's nest and then attract the hornets to the boys' bedroom. She had my full attention: the hornets nest had apparently been hanging high in an ash tree at the end of the garden – minding its own business. Suddenly, for no reason at all, it had leapt off the branch and tumbled over and over to the ground, spilling hornets out of it as it fell. They were not pleased apparently, and made a beeline (or hornet line I suppose) for the house. They had hesitated for a moment, whilst they gathered their forces together probably, and then like a flight formation of bombers shot down the chimney that led into the boys' bedroom. The boys had been lying reading on their beds, and on hearing their mothers shout to take cover, desperately hid under the bedclothes. They were unhurt apart from their bottoms – both boys had severe stings on their backsides and could hardly sit down. I was delighted, but blameless! I did think it was strange that the hornets had been so selective about their target area – I had visions of half of them holding the bedclothes up whilst the other half dropped their bombs and flew out again. I also found it rather odd that I was thought to be capable of climbing 50 feet or so up the tree, kicking the nest off and then returning to the school – all unseen and unstung.

I was not sorry to leave that foster home, and temporarily joined my mother at one of her boarding schools until another foster home could be found. I was extremely fortunate to move to another school and another foster home in Ditchling, a beautiful village in Sussex. I continued to be rather naughty, but the father of the household was endlessly patient with me and explained that I had to learn to be responsible with my power, even though I was only six.

The next three years were pretty uneventful – I spent the holidays on the whole at the foster home and attended local school with the two children. I do not really remember any startling psychic developments during this time: I was ill more often than other children – I continuously had chest or ear infections.

At nine I left the foster home as the parents were, unfortunately, splitting up and went to a boarding school for children of RAF officers in Sevenoaks. My father re-appeared, and was made Commanding Officer of another large RAF station in Suffolk, so I was sometimes treated as special at my school, probably when my father was visiting. Life continued smoothly except that I left a trail of accident-prone disasters behind me. Broken legs, arms, and ribs proceeded one after another – in fact, until I finally took control of the mind power that raged uncontrollably within me at the grand old age of fifty!

In all my mind development workshops I mention the pictures we carry in our heads of events that are usually traumatic in some way. These pictures take up a lot of memory, and often cause emotional hiccups in later life. One such event I can clearly remember. My father had come to see me and was sitting next to me in one of the pews in the beautiful old church that was attached to the school. I was very small for my age, and there was ample room for me to swing my legs; I could see the wonderful blue sky through the high window. Motes of dust drifted lazily down towards me, to disappear from sight as they left the shaft of sunlight that gently touched my knees. The church seemed like a womb – warm and dark and full of waiting. I heard the vicar from a great distance talking of the spiritual sin of being 'psychic' – of the dangers of having the sight or of being clairvoyant. I was saddened by his words, as even at nine I knew that I had abilities that were of the mind, not spiritual. I am aware that this is an extremely pat, but controversial statement. In order to develop in an orderly fashion it is most important to make this distinction. Amazingly, my father with whom I had little contact was sitting next to me. I was aware of his amusement, and in a rare moment of intimacy our eyes met with complete understanding and he gently squeezed my hand.

This is a bitter-sweet memory and it alerted me to the intolerance then shown to someone able to use these gifts. I had at the time thought that it was coincidence that my father should have visited me at my boarding school on the weekend of that particular sermon. However, a conversation overheard after the service revealed that it wasn't. When my father had been transmitting information to my mother in the war, the vicar, before he saw the light, had been one of the officers noting down the co-ordinates and composition of each airfield. After the service, I heard him comment in an undertone to his curate that he hoped that I was not contaminated with the same 'curse' as my father. I was very angry indeed, and, without further consideration sent the vicar a blinding headache for his presumption. How dare he judge us, the chosen ones! It is interesting to note that I had never even tried to do this before, but the moment I wanted to do it I could without effort. It has been this ease of access that has caused major problems to teaching others to do what I can do – if it is that easy, how do you break down the steps carried out to get there?

I remained at the boarding school until I was eleven as my mother had an operation that went wrong and was seriously ill for the next eighteen months. When she recovered, it was decided then that I should leave my school and live with my parents in Suffolk. This was the first time for years that I had lived with both, in the same house, and I attended a day school. I was not aware of being 'abnormally psychic' in any way – life for two years seemed very normal really – I continued to break the odd arm or two, cracked a rib just for good measure and sprained my ankle numerous times falling over non-existent cats.

I had been aware of the undercurrents in the house and I was not really surprised when my parents decided to separate: even now I am sad that such talented people could not live and work together to help the rest of humanity. My father, on his death bed remarked the same thing and said he wished they had tried harder. But just before my parents separated my father took me to the local air show.

It was the most spectacular show put on by an RAF station, and people came for miles to see it. We watched the planes taking off and landing in precise formation from our privileged position next to the boundary wire. After we had been watching for about an hour and my ears were ringing from the noise of the B52 bombers, my father suddenly became very still, his eyes fixed on a Valiant coming in low to land. I could feel the tension in every muscle, and even to my untutored eyes the plane seemed to be rolling a little.

I should explain here that my father had been involved in the design of the Valiant: whilst he was away on yet another mission modifications to the wing design had been made. He was aware that these changes would make the plane unstable, and indeed this proved to be the case. There was a series of fatal crashes after which the Valiant was grounded. My father kept his eyes fixed on the wings, and, holding my shoulder tight, told me to watch. As I watched, I saw what looked like a flash of lightning leave the main body of the plane and shoot down the wing. The plane stabilized and landed safely.

After the show, and with numerous ice creams and choc bars in my aching tummy, my father took me to look at the planes. When we reached the Valiant, my father whispered to me to keep silent. There were several engineers clustered round the plane looking up at the wing in astonishment and scratching their heads. From the body of the plane, out to the tip of the wing (the wings were delta shaped) there was a raised scar that looked as if someone had badly welded two parts of metal together. I have to say I was – surprised, and looked at my dad in some awe. He pressed my arm again to ensure silence, nodded pleasantly to the engineers and took me home. As we walked home, I searched desperately for the right words.

Finally, I asked him straight out if he had 'mended' the wing. He tried to explain to me about sending 'rays' out – this was in the days before lasers were commonplace – and that the mind could do this using the huge amounts of bio-electricity stored and used by our bodies. I had often wondered why my father did not mend the wing 'seamlessly' – only recently I realised it was because he wanted me to see hard evidence of what is possible, and how we can interact with our environment in an astonishing way.

Changes Again

My childhood after that was even more difficult. I attended another couple of boarding schools at which I was hardly their star pupil – I was just different. At the age of thirteen I went to a famous dancing and acting school in Sussex as I had expressed an interest in going on the stage. Just after starting on my first term I broke my leg (how surprising!) and psychosity came to rattle my cage big time. I was suspicious that things were on the move when I had the accident – I had fallen heavily whilst ice skating, having been pushed by the local thugs with my leg bent beneath me. As the attendants lifted me up, I somehow slipped through their grasp and they dropped me again – my ankle joined the breakages to my tibia and fibula. I was transported with difficult to their sick room and waited for the ambulance.

The ambulance came in due course, and as my leg was so badly broken, they carefully laid me on a wheelie bed. As they went through the heavy swing doors, grunting sand swearing they accidentally let them go and they crashed into my leg, ensuring that a couple more breaks joined my first crop.

The saga was not complete, however. I was a proficient ice skater not given to falling over, and in my pocket I had a couple of mice I had just bought from the pet shop. As I was jostled and bounced to the X ray department I suddenly remember they were still in my pocket – I just wasn't sure what state they were in. Surprisingly they were unharmed, but their effect on one of the nurses walking down the corridor in the opposite direction was like something out of a Carry On film. Her scream would have put a triumphant vampire to shame. At the same time, and I have never understood why, she threw the metal tray she was carrying, plus its contents, high into the air. Clamps, scissors, hypodermics and syringes rained down on us – I have heard of it raining cats and dogs but this was ridiculous.

The whole thing was like a scene from a science fiction film – we were all frozen in time waiting for the tray to hit the floor. When we had all regained our hearing – the tray had been spectacularly noisy – I hastily put the mice down my T-shirt and pretended nothing had happened. We marched on to the x-ray room, leaving the poor nurse incoherently talking about mice and elephants and spiders in corners. I have never really understood why!

So I arrived, plastered, at my new school. When I finally came out of my plaster ten weeks later something had changed – I became acutely aware that I could clearly see and know many of my fellow pupil's inner thoughts. Unfortunately I did not know how to hide this fact and it caused great resentment: it was of course the 'pictorial' record I saw. It is also a hard lesson to learn that just because someone asks you for the truth it doesn't mean they want to hear it. One of my class mates told her friends that I could read her insides. What a fairly horrible thought! It is important to chronicle these beginnings in order to help others see, with the wisdom of hindsight, when psychic stirrings were first felt, and how they developed before they were nipped in the bud, if indeed they were.

One episode of 'far seeing' is clearly imprinted on my memory. At the age of 13 I was still small, unpopular and not very loved. The school was housed in a beautiful building within large wooded grounds, and if I hadn't been constantly bullied I would have enjoyed myself. I would like to add here that now I am working with children I am so grateful for this experience – I can help with bullying far more effectively, having experienced it myself.

One lazy summer afternoon we were relaxing in the dormitory when the subject of clairvoyance came up. Several girls looked at me with some contempt and asked what I thought – little creep that I was. I remarked, rather rashly, that I could sometimes see the future. I offered to 'read the cards' for Diana, the most popular girl both in the dorm and in our year. She produced a pack of playing cards, then she and all her cronies gathered round me.

I realised in a panic that I could see nothing, and fearing reprisals decided to make up a story. I told her that her mother had remarried a man with the initial C and that they were going to be travelling to India together. I told her to warn them not to borrow an Austin 7 and to avoid the road to Mandalay as they might have an accident. There was a stunned silence, then she laughed derisively, told me her mother was happily married to her father whose name was Bob and ignored me for the rest of the term. Actually, that ostracism was a blessing – the tormentings and teasings stopped for several weeks.

When the summer holidays arrived my mum took me and the children from my second foster home to stay on the Isle of Wight. We had a wonderful time, and I completely forgot my words to Diana. However, when I returned to the school the next term, I was sent for by the Headmistress.

I had never been to her office before, but she had always frightened the plasters (sorry, pants) off me. I stood in her dark, wood-panelled office and wondered what on earth I had done this time. She sat behind her huge desk and peered over the top of it – she was a diminutive ex-ballerina with the presence of an empress at least. She looked at me as if I was some rather loathesome insect that had crawled out from under a stone and told me that I had been moved to a new dormitory for my own safety. Diana's mother and her lover, Chris, had been killed on the road to Mandalay in Burma when the Austin 7 they had borrowed had got a puncture and hit a tree. For the first time I realised my ability was a mixed blessing; I was also filled with horror in case I had caused the accident unintentionally. I now know, 40 years on, that I didn't cause it or 'ill-wish' Diana. There is ample evidence that it is possible to do so (gypsy curses, witch doctors etc). and indeed I studied this carefully to ensure I would never be tempted to do such things deliberately. I set up rigid 'sub-routines' that made me question my motives before letting fly with headaches or disaster.

I finally left the dancing/acting school when I was fifteen: it had a good reputation for grooming and encouraging future 'stars', and I can think of many household names who either attended at the same time or before me. Every summer a huge performance was put on – combining ballet and acting – to which a plethora of talent spotters came. Because I was the smallest in the senior school I 'landed' a part in the performance. I am sure it was with considerable trepidation that I was given a 'hang down' as opposed to a 'walk on' part. My accident-proneness was legendary – over the previous two years disaster had dogged not only my steps but the steps of anyone brave enough to walk within twenty yards of me. I think the stage managers assumed that all my disasters were deliberate and issued dire warnings of what would happen if I didn't behave myself. As most of the things they threatened me with had already been done to me by my peers, I was unfazed.

The production that year was Macbeth, a beautiful and professional production with excellent stage scenery and backdrops. I was given the part of a bat: my 'bit' involved hanging limply from the branch of a tree near the three witches as they sat on their 'blighted' moor. I would eventually have my wing nipped off for the spell. All went well at first – I kept a weather eye on the glittering and prestigious audience – but after a while I realised that I was extremely uncomfortable hanging upside down, and that all on stage were drawing their parts out so that they would be noticed. I was also bored, a fatal combination.

The witches were happily adding ingredients to their huge black cauldron. In a moment of daring I thought what fun it would be if I changed the sage into sneezing powder. Disaster followed; the witches all started to sneeze vigorously, I jumped out of my skin in astonishment and the branch on which I was hanging snapped loudly, plunging me headfirst into the cauldron. I eventually managed to extricate myself by rolling the cauldron over and backing out, bringing down the entire backdrop round us and revealing lots of scurrying people – like ants when you kick their nest. I have to admit I fled, in a most unbatlike fashion. There was complete silence for a moment, then the audience erupted. The critics said in the papers the next day that they hadn't laughed so much for years, certainly never at Macbeth, and what a brilliant production it had been. As many of the cast were offered parts or training I still can't imagine why they were so cross with me – moral: think carefully before using your mind to change things, it might work! When I was older I was shown that it is possible to change and move matter, and very easy indeed for some 'magicians' to fool the audience into believing they have done so!

After leaving that school, my unhappiness had finally been noticed by my mother, I then went to my final boarding school in Crowborough. I met the most amazing lady there who changed the course of my life. I was deeply disturbed by the time I started with her, unable to relate to anyone and very disruptive. She allowed me to sit with her in her personal study for night after night when I had my screaming nightmares. I spoke to her of the pictures I could see, of how I could change things. Of the future and how it worked, and illness. I spoke of her brother's illness – of which she knew nothing – and it was at this point that she firmly told me I had to learn to ignore the signals and signs and learn to be normal – how many times has this been said to me in my life, I wonder – if I had £10 for each time I would be very well off – but hold on a minute, what is normal anyway?

I finally left school at 16 – with my arm in plaster of course – and went to secretarial college. What a relief to be finally out in the wide, wide world and not fettered and tied to a restrictive environment!

Chapter 3

GROWING APACE – OR ONWARDS AND UPWARDS

AND SO IT WAS THAT at 16 I emerged like a shorn lamb into the wide, wide world. Of course, accidents continued to accompany me wherever I went, but I determined I would learn to be a good secretary and try to interact with my environment in a less volatile way

Once I had left school I lived with my mother 'full time' in a flat owned by a friend of hers. Probably for the first time, she realised how exhausting it is to live with a 'breaker' of things and body parts. On one famous occasion, I came off my motor bike on Hyde Park Corner and slid across six lanes of rush hour traffic: I was taken to casualty with my second set of cracked ribs that month and my first broken leg for – well, quite a long time. The first thing she said, in a resigned voice, when the hospital rang for the third time that month was "OK, what ward is she on this time?" I well remember the continuous chapter of accidents and my poor mother's despair.

I realised that although I did not have a great deal of contact in many ways with either my mum or my dad, I had nevertheless inherited their excellent access to psychic abilities on some level. One of the problems about communicating and teaching people how to develop psychic skills is that I have always had access to them and could see (but not necessarily understand) my environment in an in- depth way not granted to everyone. Even if at various points of my life I have decided to put everything on hold, I can instantly access my abilities again if necessary. It is, however, a headachesome task to try and work out how the hell I do it! Ducklings that have been brought up by chickens nevertheless eventually take nimbly to the water without tuition. There is strong evidence that many children have access to their innate psychic ability, which is then squashed out of them or repressed by either the parents or the school situation. However, my unstructured Bohemian childhood prevented this from happening and permitted psychicness to have its wicked way with me!

My mother had begun work as a spiritual healer, working with a highly respected priest at Blackfriars, called Gilbert Shaw. I'm glad to say that her training didn't really inhibit her naughtiness at all: she would inflict punctures on rude motorists, and I well remember a day when I lost several friends. We were half watching the television and there was a horse race on. My mother, whom I foolishly believed to be involved in knitting an amazing and complex jumper, looked up at the screen over the top of her glasses.

"Oh," she said dramatically, "he's so unkind to his wife – he should not be allowed to win".

The three reasonably good friends had come over prior to going out for the evening. They watched open-mouthed as Mum intervened: the jockey fell from his horse and bounced in a most satisfactory way along the grass. I tried to explain to her that this was rather reprehensible (I think that's the word!); she smiled sweetly at me and agreed. She died at the end of 1999, and it is only after her death that I realise how multi-talented she was, and how lonely it must have been for her to have abilities that were frowned on in her faith, and not to have been able to develop in the more open environment of our society today. She could do so many things – always win a draw or lottery, detect illness in people, know the life history of complete strangers and many other strange phenomena!

It was shortly after my adventure with a bus, a taxi, two bicycles and a pushchair (empty, luckily) that my mother decided I had run headlong into disaster for long enough, and that she ought to ask for help. She took me to meet Father Shaw when I was 18. He had helped her both with her spiritual and mental development, and she hoped he might help me to become less uncontrolled. As I stood in front of Father Shaw, I was immediately struck by the power I could feel from him... All the defences I had erected to protect me from being seen as different came tumbling down. He was an austere, white-haired man, with no time for pretence. He looked at me gravely for several minutes without speaking, then, taking the pipe out of his mouth, he told me to sit down. He warned me that I had great mind power, which could be misused and that when I had developed it fully I should not become a 'showman' at a psychic circus. He said he wished such power had been given to someone steadier and less flashy than myself, and that he feared for my future if I didn't learn some self-control and stop abusing my environment. This was the first time the connection between my accident-proneness and uncontrolled mental power had been made, and I only remembered these words 30 years later when I came to the same conclusion myself!

Father Shaw again looked at me in silence for a minute – I felt like a particularly large and squashy maggot on a piece of cheese - then he gave me a demonstration of what the mind could do. He had a surprisingly garish mug on his table, more suited, one felt, to a seaside fortune-telling booth than to the office of an elder in the church. He told me to watch the mug carefully. The mug rose into the air like a harrier jet, and then descended back to the table. My mouth of course dropped down round my ankles like a hungry daffodil: Father Shaw continued to look at me steadily. "Mhairi, watch carefully." The mug rose into the air again and then returned to the table – but it wasn't the same thing.

Desperately, I tried to work out what the difference was. Father Shaw waited patiently, smoking his huge pipe. Finally, with his first smile since meeting me, he explained that he had done two different things – once he had actually raised the mug, once he had told my mind he had raised the mug but he hadn't. Many hypnotists have perfected this technique. He then said that one day, if and when I became a mature psychic, I would know which was real and which wasn't. Hooray, now I do! Maturity at last. As I have said, Father Shaw was the first person I had met who made the differentiation between mental psychic ability and spiritual intuition and input, and made me aware of my own power and its potential destructiveness.

The great man had watched me whilst all these bewildering thoughts and emotions crossed my mind. Finally, he turned gravely to my mother and told her he felt my psychic growth should be kept under control until I could manage things better. Looking at him with great trust, she slowly nodded. He leant forward, placed his hands on my head, closed his eyes and spoke several words in a language I didn't recognise. Just before we left, I had a slight headache but that was all. The 'mental cap', which he placed over my psyche, remained in place until I finally had it removed during a healing session. Unfortunately, this cap had absolutely no effect on the disasters that continued to afflict me – but I'm sure it prevented the uncontrolled use of my abilities until I was more responsible. Fortunately, I didn't have to wait for that, or I would be an old lady in a wheel chair happily clicking my false teeth.

The removal of the cap was like something out of one of the gorier torture chamber scenes during the Spanish Inquisition. I have a good friend, Julian, who is a healer. We spend many a long hour arguing out the finer points of healing. It was while we were discussing the healing of the mind that I got a severe headache that lasted five minutes then vanished. When Julian laid hands on my head we both had clear 'mind pictures' of the silver cap. Until that moment, I had completely forgotten its existence. Over the years, the cap had worn thin in places, permitting 'weeds' to push through. With intense concentration, Julian prayed for me, at the same time as pulling the cap upwards with his mind. This is rather like trying to remove chicken wire from the grip of nettles and grass. After it was done, and the cap removed, I bled profusely from every orifice and felt desperately ill for several days. I also became aware that I could sense and see things more clearly.

I feel incredibly privileged to have met Father Shaw – although I didn't think so at the time. Just after that meeting, I met another amazing man who gave me much of the spiritual learning I have today: if I had not been such a gadfly at 18 (and 19, 20, 21 – ..) I would have learnt much more from our encounters.

Dom Robert Petit-Pierre was an Anglican monk specialising in exorcism of environments and people. He saw the same problems that Father Shaw had seen – that I was a giddy gadfly (I don't actually know what that is, but it puts the picture across) - but his approach to me was slightly different: he decided to train me and show me the spiritual path and familiarise me with other dimensions, so that I could protect myself. He was a gentle, kind man but a hard taskmaster. One would expect such a spiritual giant to be awe-inspiring on the physical level as well.

Dom Robert was one of the most unwell people I have ever met: he had kidney problems, was very short sighted indeed and was an acute diabetic. I well remember when he was interviewed on a chat show. He sat there in his shabby monk's habit, smiling gently. The chat show host asked him about his work, and then remarked that surely if he followed God and did His will he should expect healing of all his physical problems.

Dom Robert leant back, steepling his fingers together. "Look at me," he said. "How can I in my weak physical state possibly cast out demons and carry out exorcisms? As it is, all glory must go to God." The interviewer was silenced. Like me, he was overcome by the greatness of Dom Robert. He leant across and very gently patted Dom Robert's knee in a gesture of complete support.

One of the main reasons I stress the importance of keeping spiritual and mental psychic development separate is because both Gilbert Shaw and Dom Robert believed this was vital. Both men were extremely self-disciplined – both emphasised to me that I must take control of both elements, and keep them separate. As they were both so effective in their respective fields I listened to them and I was taught so much.

As part of my training, Dom Robert took me with him to visit various houses and people that were possessed. He would speak quietly, but with authority, to whatever entity was trapped in this dimension and help it to return from whence it came. He always used the same rituals – the same preparations - and when I speak to many people involved in this same field today I am shocked at the sloppiness of the approach. He would never make a visit without the backing prayers of the other monks in his monastery: he carried holy water and salt (I could see a blue light playing round the salt when he showed it to me). Recently, inspired by Dom Robert's work, I have started a survival course for people who travel "astrally" without being properly prepared.

Dom Robert died when I was 21, and I put all the things I had learnt from him on the back burner for future reference, and then continued to interact in an abusive way with my environment – broken ribs, a doddle: broken arm, par for the course, broken leg, normal occurrence.

My mother decided when I was in my late teens that it was time I had a bit of culture in my life, and learned how the other 'arf lived. I joined a frightfully smart club in the West End and tried to learn how to be terribly posh. I was, in fact asked to leave, as it was felt I was too destructive to be a member. I really cannot imagine why they took this high-handed attitude – the curtains I had accidentally burnt were of course incredibly expensive to replace, but were insured. The pale cream carpet I spilt red wine and cream on could be sorted – after all, they charged enough to be a member, and the MP I had knocked out whilst waving my arms about madly (demonstrating a stroke in tennis) had eventually recovered.

I think in fact it was the Christmas ball, to which even minor royals came, that led to my banishment. The enormous hall in which the ball was held was reached by the most impressive staircase I have ever seen. As each guest arrived, they were announced in loud and pompous tones by the major domo. The guest then majestically descended the stairs, watched by the people who had already arrived. My turn came. I was determined to be majestic too. As I began to walk down the stairs, my high heel broke off. Desperately I clutched the bannister rail to steady myself. The hood of my beautiful evening dress caught on the huge ball of wood at the top of the bannister rail: with a tearing, rending noise that sounded as if the gates of hell had been opened, my dress gave up the uneven battle and I left it hanging like a limp flag whilst I continued down the stairs on my bottom in my underwear. This time I didn't laugh – I cried. With a sweet smile, one of the royals took off his jacket and put it round me. I was and am so grateful – what a caring thing to do.

Stablity, at Last!

My mother gave up on me after that (I was obviously never going to turn into a beautiful cultured pearl) and so did most of my boyfriends: frankly, they couldn't cope with the eventfulness of our times together. I did, however, finally marry and had my wonderful and long-suffering family. We stayed with friends until I had my first daughter, then we moved into the semi-derelict house in West Kensington we had bought – all that we could afford. The house was on four floors, including a basement, and the only part that was habitable was the basement and first floor – in which we had sitting tenants. I was now in my element – legitimate destruction. I was allowed to knock down walls and ceilings, or at least some of them. I still laugh when I remember that whilst I was vastly pregnant with my second daughter I had been hoovering under the sloping eaves in a very small space, my stomach hanging down between the rafters. My daughter, Rebeccah, then decided she was feeling rather cramped and decided to move, efficiently trapping my stomach between the rafters I pushed and pulled – my stomach was stuck like a cork in a bottle. I was acutely aware that my husband was busy plastering the ceiling in the room below, and that he was not very efficiently supervising my first daughter. I saw her quite clearly in my mind heading for the open window in the bathroom, 40 feet up from the ground.

There was a squelchy plop as I finally disentangled my stomach and scuttled to the middle of the roof where I could just about stand. So intent was I on reaching my daughter, Faith, that I didn't even hear my husband's despairing cries as my feet appeared like inverted footprints in the snow in the ceiling below. How I didn't break one if not both my legs as they sunk between the rafters I shall never know. I arrived at the bathroom just as Faith was triumphantly climbing out on the windowsill.

Then I noticed the silence from the sitting room and, clutching Faith firmly under one arm, peeped round the corner. My husband was staring, speechless, at the ruin of his ceiling. I tiptoed away – discretion being the better part of valour!

I gave birth to my daughter that night – I think she had decided she was sick of being whooshed about like a sea horse in a turbulent sea and was making a break for it. Surprisingly I had her easily – almost too easily. I had been having misgivings earlier on in the evening, and kept thinking about shooting stars and fast flowing rapids.

When I went into labour I was aware almost at once that Rebeccah, having made up her mind that now was the time for her entry, was impatient. We screamed round the corners on our way to the hospital like Starsky and Hutch and arrived with a squeal of brakes like a nest of angry pigs. I was escorted hurriedly to the labour room. An hour later, crossing my legs like a constipated dinosaur, I hauled myself out of the labour room where I had been lying in state, and two-stepped out into the corridor. When I see one of the adverts for a courier company, I am strongly reminded of that moment: I was quite unable to get someone to help me deliver my parcel. I tried a subtle whisper, asking for help, then my more imperative ringing tones, finally a shout that rattled all the windows in the corridor. That brought 'em.!! Several staff nurses came rushing towards me, reproaching me for all the noise. I explained that I was about to drop my baby in the corridor, and that I was not sure how well they bounced when they were newly born.

Crossly they helped me onto a trolley, muttering about troublemakers, when Rebeccah arrived with all the subtlety of a shell fired across enemy lines. They almost gave me a sedative I laughed so much – it was so comical to see the three staff nurses crouching at the end of the trolley to field the baby, closely followed, at the same velocity, by the after birth. I suggested they would be an asset to a rugger scrum but they were not very amused. Rebeccah is the child who has psychic 'leanings' but fights it tooth and nail. She can – although she shouldn't have been able to of course – clearly describe one of the three nurses who delivered her. This astounding fact came up in conversation:

I mentioned that she had not been a beautiful baby when she was born, and she remarked that at least she hadn't caught (like an infectious disease) the problems of one of the nurses: she didn't have a nose with a large wart on it and a voice like a gravel machine. When she said that the memory came flooding back. I remembered that poor nurse who had a voice like a corncrake and a wart from hell. Having fielded Rebeccah, she went off duty and I didn't see her again.

I returned home in a couple of days - I was in the peak of health and ready for the next part of our work programme. Whilst I had been away my husband had been painting the hall – it looked beautiful. I climbed up on the scaffold board to have a wider view. When we had first seen the house the beautiful stained glass fanlight in the front door had been the deciding factor in taking on such a huge venture. My husband had covered the fanlight with paper to stop it being splattered with paint. I carefully removed the paper to improve the light. As I did so, the whole thing fell out of its frame and on to the pavement below, nearly decapitating our cat. I didn't need to hear the huge crash to know that the window had gone to be part of the great greenhouse in the sky. Without a word, my husband handed me back Rebeccah and stalked upstairs.

Life continued much as it had prior to Rebeccah's arrival. I was a lot more tired, working in the evenings after a day with two children under three: I still did my bit. One night, the second very funny incident happened. I was trying to re-cement some bricks that had become loose after I removed the plaster. I was working away when one of the bricks suddenly vanished through the party wall.

Our next door neighbour was a bit of a Lothario (loads a birds) and was sitting listening to some mood-inducing music whilst entwined with his latest conquest. On his side of the party wall was a decorative hearth, fashionably laid with pine cones and twigs. I realised I had to get the brick back, and reached through the hole to find it, questing here and there with my hand.

There was a piercing scream from next door, which nearly gave me a heart attack, and I could hear footsteps running across the floor, down the stairs and out of the front door. When she was safely out of the house, she shouted up at the window that she should never have cheated on her husband, and that she hadn't realised that the Addams family was based on fact. I had a strong feeling that 'hand' would not have been so soot covered as it went about its business.

My next door neighbour was a little peeved, but as he hadn't realised his victim was married felt it was all for the good. Just before he moved, he confessed that he had always suspected I was a witch (no idea why) and that he always checked to see if I was flying round in the sky before he went to bed. After that the house continued to improve and my children survived being fed with one arm whilst the other was in plaster. Faith learnt to carry Rebeccah carefully when I broke three ribs falling over the cat (I don't think he had forgiven me for the fanlight episode and had been waiting for vengeance!)

I became more and more aware that I see the pictures that people carried and that I often could see both their past and their (potential) futures. Once my children were reasonably mobile, I decided that I should offer my services at the church we had always attended in West Kensington. One of the big plus sides of this was that I found an acceptable way of accessing and using the power I had put on the back burner. I took over one of the three Sunday Schools operating whilst the parents were in church, and I also helped to run a youth club. I was able, legitimately, to reveal that I could see events that would affect the church: I did not however reveal that I could also see the mind-pictures the children carried and help them to deal with their fears. It was also here that I began to develop techniques to help the children protect themselves from physical danger whilst they travelled to and from their youth meetings. These techniques were refined over the passage of time and are given later in the book.

I could also see the past - I could help people in the church come to terms with past hurt and take effective action to deal with it. This ability to deal compassionately but powerfully with problems is innate in us all and allows us to move our lives forward instead of dwelling in and re-living the past.

My children were inextricably woven into my continuingly adventuresome life, as were the various children that came to live with us for varying amounts of time. We moved from our first house just before my son was born – I continued to break limbs with monotonous regularity, found that road works had a way of collapsing round me as I passed, and For Sale boards had a penchant for rapping me smartly on the head as they practised being kites in a thunderstorm.

Once my first two children started school, mishaps multiplied like fertile rabbits. A new windscreen a month was the norm, but two the more usual. I had punctures regularly, and was regularly given tickets for parking on double yellow lines whilst waiting for the rain to stop so that I could change the wheel. I had a friendly tyre replacement and puncture repairer locally, and he even came to court to bear witness to the fact that my inner tyre tubes were like patchwork quilts. With the change of law about punctures and tyre replacement, I would nowadays be responsible for the complete destruction of every rubber tree in the Far East. My children were stoical, and accepted the downs with the downs (sorry, ups with the downs).

I remember once, when yet again I was late for school with my children because of yet another puncture (the third that week), I apologised (again) to the headmaster. He was an amazingly humorous and kindly man, although a stickler for discipline. Looking at me with a smile he remarked, "My dear, if you arrived and told me that you had parked near the North End Road and an elephant had sat on the car and squashed it, I would believe it". I was a little bemused by this, but when a concrete mixer truck dumped a load of concrete on my car, completely burying the front, I told the headmaster, as I made my breathless way into the school, that I would rather it had been an elephant, as clearing the concrete had been such a nightmare.

I think the trail of disasters that followed me like orphaned lambs were due to the suppression of the mind power that I should have been using – my body had become bloated with power and my less than occasional incidents with cars, motor bikes, in the house, and so on, were due to 'electrical' constipation.

It is amazing how time lends mellowness to the incidents that clamour in my mind for attention.... One nightmare journey with four children, two cats, three dogs, a hen, two rabbits and two guinea pigs in the car springs to mind as eventful. The puncture was quickly dealt with - I had vast experience of changing wheels by the time my first child was six months old. The windscreen proved more of a problem. As I looked round at my children's glum faces (the animals were all being held on laps to save space) I prayed hard that it wouldn't rain, that the AA would come quickly and that the animals would not escape. My middle daughter, Rebeccah, a sunny little girl of nine, remarked wistfully that it was a pity we had given the rabbits a drink before we left. I looked at her in amazement. "But you're not even holding them, darling."

"I know," she replied, even more sadly, "that's what I mean

about a drink." The overpowering smell of rabbit problems was to some extent lost by the extra air intake from the non-existent windscreen.

When the AA arrived - some considerable time later, having gone to the wrong location - the rain had washed most of our problems away. We waited whilst he fitted a new windscreen, multiple sneezes issuing from the wet children in the back. At last we were on our way.

The second puncture was more of a problem... we had no spare wheel. The officious motorway patrolman left with a large flea in his ear when he foolishly remarked I should carry a spare. Eventually, the AA arrived again. By this time, my oldest daughter, Faith, was remarking that she wished she lived with a normal family who did not have disasters on every outing, that did not have quite so many animals with such a volume of excreta, and whose baby brothers were not sick all over their sisters' knees. I had considerable sympathy for her, as I had a large bite on my neck from one of the rabbits that had been making for the open window. It was whilst the patrolman was changing the tyre that the cats decided that they had had enough. With a heart wrenching moan that would do credit to a dying dinosaur, both of them had diarrhoea over the other occupants of the car.

We were now on our way. "Let's sing a song." I said cheerfully. There was a stunned silence from the back. Faith returned to the attack.

"Mother" she said from the superiority of her 11 years, "we have been sicked on, crapped on, scratched; we are tired, hungry and thirsty, and you suggest we sing..."

Having started, she couldn't stop. An entire catalogue of the disasters that occurred on most days of our lives was begun.

"Every journey we have at least one puncture, often two. We have witnessed traffic accidents of every kind, broken down regularly, been attacked by a dog that bit the tyres and burst them, roads have been closed as we arrive at them."

I had by then ceased to listen. She would get over it, probably. In fact, a battle royal ensued, as all four children argued about what sort of dog it was that had attacked our tyres. My son, James, reckoned it was a corgi, and rolled up his trousers to show the battle scars on his ankles to prove the size of the dog's teeth. I was horrified and nearly drove off the road as I realised that even at five years old, he was so used to being attacked and damaged by his environment that he didn't even bother to mention it any more.

The journey home was not complete, however. What should have been a three-hour journey had already taken six when the headlights went out. This time there were no comments from the back. Everyone was asleep, completely exhausted. two hours later, we proceeded on our way home, to arrive ten hours after our departure from Norfolk. I shudder as I remember unloading the car and its scratching, biting occupants. I did not bathe the animals - it would have been an all night job – but I did bathe the children.

I saw my nephew, the fourth child, who used to stay with us regularly, the other day.

"Do you remember that nightmare journey back from Norfolk?" I asked him fondly. He looked at me with puzzlement for a minute.

"Which particular journey do you mean?" he asked me at last. "Didn't that sort of thing happen every journey?"

I was silenced!

It was whilst my children were still quite young that I realised, in a more definite way, that there is a difference between a mind psychic approach and a spiritual one. I used to visit a healing mission in London as I was trying to develop my ability to be an effective healer. Whilst I was there, I met a young drug addict who was trying to kick his habit so that he could start to function again. I was appalled when he was told to leave the Mission, but that he could come back once he had kicked his habit. I really wanted to help him and started to visit him at home. He lived with his devoted and amazing wife in Brixton, in a block of flats.

His wife was one of the most courageous people I have ever met. She believed in her husband absolutely, and that he could kick his habit. I also believed he could, and was sure, as I had witnessed how my mother could change things, that I could change how his drugs acted on his body: actually, rather a large conclusion to come to. There is a difference between knocking jockeys off their horses and altering the biochemistry of the human body.

I was very inexperienced at this point, may I say in my defence – now I would be a little more subtle! As I looked at him - a truly beautiful man wrecked by his addiction - I asked him if he was sure he wanted to kick his drugs, as what I was going to do for him was permanent. After some hesitation, he agreed. Thinking hard for a moment, I made the necessary alterations to his biochemistry. Nearly 18 years later, I still cannot tell you how I did this. Perhaps it was beginners luck, I don't know: but it was, of course, a foolish thing to do. Because his biochemistry was changed, he could not even benefit from painkillers – they just didn't work any more. I did not tell Lucas, the young man, what I had done, but just told him to watch for the results. The following day I had a desperate phone call.

"What on earth have you done?" he asked me sadly. "I still want the drugs, but I have taken large amounts of Heroin with no effect at all. I've even tried different dealers!"

I was delighted, and told him so. He was – less pleased. Not an ideal solution and I was too stupid to realise it at that point! Another very good reason to help my clients take control of their own powers, rather than rely on my largesse.

I must admit I thought very little about this afterwards, until I had a phone call from Lucas's wife. She was beside herself. Lucas had been admitted to hospital with gangrenous leg ulcers, a common side effect of mainlining drug abuse. Both legs were to be amputated the following day. I rushed to the hospital as fast as I could. I spent some time using my mind to check out what was happening, and then about an hour praying for him and giving him some healing. By God's great mercy, the following day his ulcers had disappeared and he was discharged from the hospital. I had helped him by using my mind to unblock some of the local blood vessels, but the main healing was directly from God. I think what impressed Lucas most (he was so frightened of me that he could not bear to see me after this) was that the surgeon remarked to him, "God obviously has a very special purpose for you young man." He is now a vicar with a ministry to drug addicts.

In any situation, particularly where there are serious health issues, spiritual healing and psychic power should work side by side. A profundity I was quite incapable of working out at that point, but which I have now come to realise is true.

Because my children were not yet adult, I decided to limit my activities and exploits in the wide world and concentrate on them. We stumbled on, my family and I, through every kind of disaster. I realised how very fed up my children were when, in their late teens, they took me on one side before we went out for a celebration meal and begged me not to spill tomato ketchup over our table and everyone else's, not to knock our table over (or indeed anyone else's) and definitely not to break the loo again or we would not be allowed to return.

I think all my family breathed a sigh of relief when I finally returned to full-time employment and the responsibility for my behaviour passed on to someone else!

Chapter 4

CAREER, HERE I COME

I SUPPOSE I HAD HOPED THAT when I returned to full time work, the trail of accidents and disasters would finally peter out – perhaps unsurprisingly, they didn't: I still had not begun a self-disciplined approach to my powers. All that happened was that my victims changed.

I applied for a lowly job as a Curator Grade G, doing temporary work with a heritage body in March 1986: foolishly, you might well say, they employed me. I was extremely nervous at the interview, having flattened one of the interview panel when I charged through the door a little late for my appointment. I had picked her up, patted her roughly back into shape, and then registered my arrival at the information desk. I entered the interview room and immediately spotted my erstwhile victim.

Most of the panel were very typically civil service, I think – conservatively dressed, serious in a civil service way, and guarded in a civil service way. My boss-to-be, Stephanie, was like a shaft of sunshine in that austere civil service room – she is a wonderful woman and during the years I worked for her, she supported me to the hilt. She is fair-haired, very pretty (my husband tells me), with a wonderful smile. She told me afterwards that the rest of the panel were unconvinced of my suitability – after all, I had blurted out the reason for my lateness. I had arrived by motorbike, but I couldn't park, as all the bays were full, so I parked on a parking meter. As I had no change, I organised the meter so that it would continue to show three minutes credit until I returned. As I explained this to them, their bewildered expressions told me I had made a slight mistake in giving them this juicy morsel.

Incidentally, this is one of the easiest and naughtiest things to do: when I think about how I did it I am really not sure – did I jam the meter (very illegal and probably bad for the meter), did I somehow insert time instead of money (I like that explanation), or did I delude the traffic Mafiosi into misreading the meter? (I like that the best – I am not particularly fond of this species of people.) Anyway, to my astonishment, I got the job. Despite my continuing trail of 'problems' involving most of the people round me, most of the time, I progressed. Within two years, I was Queen of the Microfilm programme, Supremo of the Photographic Library (90,000 images waiting for disaster to strike) and Mafia boss of the public enquiry desk for the Archaeology Section. I don't think I made these wonders happen, but I do occasionally ponder it – I was like a meteor ploughing across the heavens, scattering stars in my wake. I don't think the stars woke up until I had progressed even further into the echelons of famedom (oh dear, I digress again). For whatever reason I made it!

As part of my rising star status, I regularly gave talks to some of our most august organisations – the British Library, the Society of Archivists and various other bodies. One particular talk stands out in my mind – it was my first and could easily have been my last. I was talking to the students of one of the London art colleges about the use of microfilm in archives. I looked at the sea of bored faces, and thought about how to convert them to my cause. I was actually looking quite smart for a change and felt ready to tackle anything – oh, foolish woman! In ringing tones I exhorted the students to hear my words, to really listen, and the microphone packed up in an impressive cloud of sparks. I told them to see past the wonders of modern technology, and the inoffensive computer-generated image projected on to the screen behind me disappeared, as the computer gave up the ghost with a big bang.

I'm sometimes a little slow in the uptake – I really did not notice my audience's response to the microphone episode. I did, however, see the consternation on most faces as the computer died, and when in even louder ringing tones – I after all had to reach the back of the auditorium – I mentioned that I wanted them to remember my words when I was no longer with them, there was a frantic stampede to leave the auditorium. I think There was a universal premonition about what would happen next. Hardly had I finished speaking when the entire Podium on which I was standing disintegrated, projecting me forcefully into the bowels of the earth.

I was a little stunned at all the visual aids I had called up – but not very surprised when the college did not ask me to repeat my lecture for the next year's students. Foolishly again, I mentioned this episode, with a hearty laugh, whilst I was talking to the organiser of the Annual Conference of the Society of Archivists, at which I was a speaker. He had been regarding me in an avuncular, happy way, gently sipping his pint of beer. When I told him the story, and he considered the implications for his precious conference, he went an interesting shade of green – he looked a little like a sad gooseberry. I received my come-uppance – throughout my serious and learned talk the organiser scurried at regular intervals from the back to worriedly examine the stage, check the wires to all the equipment and measure with his steel rule to see if there was any evidence of sinkage in the podium on which I was standing. All this was accompanied by incoherent muttering – like the white rabbit in Alice in Wonderland – the whole thing was most disconcerting!

My life really did seem to be a succession of accidents whilst I was with the organisation in London (prior to relocation in 1994). Telephone directories were dropped on my head and, in one remarkable incident, I closed a major London street for half an hour. I had been to collect 5,000 A4 plastic folders for our paper archives. Just as I was about to cross the road, the bottom dropped out of both the extra strong carrier bags I was carrying. A sea of plastic spread generously across the entire width of the street. A policeman, on traffic duty, stopped the traffic and organised 'volunteers' to help me pick up the folders: this was easier said than done, as it was rather like trying to put a bandage on an electric eel – the folders had a life of their own. Eventually, red faced with exertion, we managed to control them by wrapping them up in the evening papers the policeman commandeered from a news vendor. When I have my bad dream nights, I can see the long line of people, looking like refugees from some major disaster, walking to the head office with folders clasped to their breasts, and then handing them to the staff on the enquiry desk. Once released from captivity the folders again took on a life of their own and wriggled frantically out of the papers as soon as they were put down.

Accidents never come in ones, do they? I'm just not sure why they have to come in nineteens, or twenties or – sorry, I digress. The next day, I resolved I would be more careful – but.... I was responsible for the collection of excavation microfilms – its curation, filing and so on. Many of us are familiar with these sheets of reduced photographic images – the libraries use them to list books, and motor factors use them to list parts. As part of the security procedures to ensure the longevity of the microfilmed information, a master copy – never really handled after filing – and back-up copies were kept in an environmentally controlled atmosphere. On this particular day I had collected a drawer of back-up microfiches from the basement and was carrying them up stairs. On the last step, I tripped. The microfiche shot out of the drawer over the banisters and down the stairwell. I could hear people cursing as the film landed on their heads or where they were just about to tread. As we were due a visit from one of the government ministers, I was not popular – especially with the head of section. At that time he was also my line manager, and in that role he had tried several times to put a damage limitation on me, especially after I had nearly strangled the Chairman in the laminator.

What a wonderful man the chairman was: one of the kindest

and cleverest people I have ever met – a gentle giant. He said so little in recrimination when I hastily cut his tie off, as he headed head first for the rollers. He looked very sad and said it had been his best old school tie. I smiled brightly and told him that now at least it was preserved for posterity – When I thought how nearly his posterior had been preserved as well, I hastily changed the subject. I did actually feel very guilty.

After the microfiche incident, my boss sent for me: I could tell he was seriously peeved. He looked at me coldly and asked me what was next on the menu. I had just come out of plaster, having been knocked off my motorbike by a car coming against the traffic lights down a one way street the wrong way. The policeman on duty outside the American Embassy had seen it and congratulated me on doing the job thoroughly. As there was a traffic jam, the motorist had not disappeared. The policeman hared across to the car. He returned, white-faced with anger. "I shall be making a report," he said, "but she's a diplomat and claiming diplomatic immunity." Her particular government is notorious for not contributing when there is an accident.

For a moment, the landscape appeared in black and white before me. Angrily I threw a major headache to the woman, and for good measure a puncture in both her back wheels. While writing this book, my co-writer has been trying to wean me off this habit, but I *do* find it hard. Justice must be done.

I departed via ambulance to my local hospital. It was only months later that I bumped into my nice young policeman again.... He stopped me to tell me that the woman had been summoned back to her own country, not for having damaged my wonderful body, but because she had knocked over one of the high-ups when she suddenly had two punctures. As the man had only had two broken fingers, I thought that was a poor exchange for my leg.

I returned to the present with a jump and looked at my head of section, a stickler for normality and convention. I hoped he did not know – and never would – of the cup of coffee incident, or of the telephone directories. After looking at me in silence for a moment, he steepled his fingers together.

"I know about the telephone directories, the cup of coffee, the game of rounders and of course, the plastic folders. None of these directly affect our good name, so we shall ignore them for now."

I waited tensely in my chair to be dismissed from the royal presence, when he continued speaking, still staring out of the window. "But why?" he asked.

Fortunately the telephone rang at this point, and I escaped with great speed.

I retired to the ladies and tried to prepare my answers for Alan – he was sure to follow up at some point. The telephone directories had been gratuitous violence, as far as I was concerned. What business had they to fall on my head just after I had taken my motorcycle helmet off? Why should the parking bay have been underneath a window against which the directories had been placed? And why indeed had the office manager chosen that moment to throw his illegal cigarette out of the window, dislodging the books?

As I lay stunned on the ground, our personnel manager came past. He picked me up, dusted me down, and escorted me in to the office building. "We'll meet again," he said prophetically.

And indeed we did. My office was on the second floor of a building faced in the front by a very busy road in the West End and at the back by a smaller street, used as a short-cut, so the traffic is continuous and noisy. One very hot day, I was bored and thought how nice it would be if the streets were quieter, cars and buses stopped rushing past on the main road, and that the street behind the building would become a ghost town and people would not come into the public enquiry section, so that I could justify going over the road for a coffee.

I didn't at first notice that the streets had fallen silent – the only noise was the sound of a road drill somewhere behind me. Idly I looked out of the window. No traffic in the front, no traffic at the back. Yippee, thought I. I rushed down the stairs and charged into the coffee bar opposite. The coffee bar was empty. I asked what had happened. The owner, a cheerful Italian with a sad face like a bloodhound, told me there had been a bomb scare and the streets were now cordoned off. At the same time there was a suspected gas leak nearby and they had shut the road for emergency repairs. I looked at him open-mouthed, then inspiration struck.

Within five minutes, a rollicking game of rounders was in full swing outside the office building and across the road. My small game to beat boredom had turned into a major match. Never was there such a cross section of people: several high ups from another heritage body, three commissionaires, two people from the hairdressers opposite, two from the coffee bar and two policemen from the local station. We would have continued longer if the Chief Superintendent hadn't appeared. I was left holding the baby – or baseball bat. "Good afternoon," he remarked pleasantly. "I hope you are enjoying your game of hopscotch." I looked at him a little warily...maybe the bomb scare had turned his brain. He winked at me, and sauntered on to the Station.

I was sitting, yet again, in the Personnel Officer's office. He was looking at me, as usual, rather humorously. I thought I might as well come clean, and tell him of all (or most!) of the latest mishaps: I diffidently mentioned the rounders game, playing down the rollicking nature of the whole thing. My conscience pricked me and I decided I'd better confess.

"I only thought how nice it would be if it was quieter round here," I began defensively. "I don't think...well, I caused anything to happen." (Like the abortive bomb scare or the false alarm about the gas leak, or indeed the train problems being experienced locally). From his very startled expression I could see that until that moment he hadn't considered that aspect either. He looked very thoughtful afterwards, however.

I thought I shouldn't give him any more time to ponder the implications of what I'd said and rushed on to talk about the coffee incident. In fact, it really isn't funny at all, but everybody I have told the story is – very unkindly – extremely amused.

I had gone to get a cup of coffee on my way in to work. As I stepped off the pavement I tripped. The coffee left the plastic cup and in a perfect arc took itself gleefully through a passing taxi window to land on the passenger's unsuspecting knees. With a scream that would have done credit to a tortured banshee he leapt from his seat, frantically brushing his trousers... the taxi then, fortunately for me, bore him away. I was just about to make my guilty dash across the road when there was a tap on my shoulder.

"Wonderful," enthused the man behind me, "Could you do that again? I'm a journalist and involved in video coverage: we could film it next time."

I just stood gawping at him. Not waiting for a reply, he continued, patting all his cameras, lenses, films, etc. that were festooned round him like baubles on a Christmas tree

"But how on earth did you put the coffee through a window that is only open two inches, without spilling any of it on the window? How did you select your victim?" I put my hands over my ears and fled.

The Personnel Officer sat in silence, carved from stone. "I think we won't mention that story, don't you?" was all he said.

I stood up, interview over, consumed with guilt again. Poor young man, probably on his way to a job interview with various and sundry burns and wet drawers.

As I have said, accidents get lonely on their own and have to enlist help from their friends. Just after all my office-related traumas, the disaster area moved to my domestic arena. I met a mallard duck – or rather, the mallard duck met me. I had the day off from work and had just dropped off my son at school and was travelling in Richmond Park, enjoying a beautiful, mellow autumn drive, when I heard a strange noise from the back of my car: I got out to investigate (poor sap that I am): a careful examination of each wheel failed to reveal any problems, but as I stood up from checking the last wheel, a duck fell on my head. As I gently stroked the poor dead Mallard, feeling not a little stunned, a parks policeman tapped me on the shoulder. I turned to him, blood pouring down my face from the cut from the duck's beak.

Foolishly, I thought he would mop my brow and pat me kindly on the shoulder and be generally kind. I thought wrong. He firmly removed the duck from my arms, informing me that I couldn't keep it – that was poaching, and anyway would I move along, as I was not allowed to park there. He then returned to his motorbike and roared off. I thought some of the more extreme fascist organisations of the past had missed out on a good recruit.

I must admit I was a little surprised at this incident, and decided as I made my way to my local hospital – again – I would not tell them how I had been injured. All was well, at first. I explained that I had banged my head on a cupboard. Two stitches and a head x-ray later – I had chipped the bone in my left eyebrow – I prepared to leave Casualty. As I was leaving, I noticed that a friend of mine had come on duty at reception. She asked me what on earth had happened. I explained to her very quietly how a duck had fallen on my head. From behind her a head popped up – one of the junior doctors had been filing some reports and overheard my explanation. With a speed that would have done credit to Roger Bannister, he disappeared back into casualty. I heard him telling the other doctors what had happened, and then heard gales of laughter.

I was just about to beat a hasty retreat when Sister Casualty appeared like an avenging angel. She was a small woman, but appeared at least twice life size as she stormed up to me.

"Get out of my department," she said, pointing dramatically to the exit. "You have made my dangerously ill patients laugh. One of my men on a life support machine nearly fell off the bed...go." I went.

The interesting sequel to this story is that when a TV crew made a documentary about the incident it was also beset with problems. The director had visited my old office two years after I left. He had taken one of my friends out for a drink to thank her for all the trouble she had gone to in searching for information. In passing, he had remarked that he was doing a documentary on accident prone people – especially when the accidents involved animals! My friend – along with a group of other staff who were in the pub – dissolved into hysterical laughter and they all collapsed in a heap as they vied with one another to recount all the disasters that had occurred whilst I was still with them. One of the most amusing parts of the reconstruction was of my arrival at the main entrance of the hospital on my way to the A & E department. The director had allowed fifteen minutes for his crew to follow my progress into the building. An hour and a half later, he was nearly tearing his hair out.

"Would you tell all those people who keep on stopping to help you and escort you to Casualty that no one cares about anyone else today. People just don't behave like that any more."

Actually, I couldn't quite believe it either – my stage blood was not even very obvious. I apologised profusely for his problems – after all, I spent my entire life saying sorry to my victims and to lamp post, trees, walls – and eventually had to scuttle in a most undignified way from the road and into the entrance like some mysterious celebrity on her way to a film matinee.

Relocation Blues

In fact, the duck incident seemed to move me into the animal incident arena coinciding with my organisation relocating to Swindon. I was responsible for the safe (!) carriage of a number of very important paper archives connected with excavations in England: I think our clients were blissfully unaware of my history, and indeed I must stress that the archives were never damaged whilst in my care. On one very interesting day I was bowling along happily to work in the office car having picked up and delivered sundry items to our microfilming bureaux. I was just overtaking a juggernaut travelling in the inside lane when I noticed a falcon fluttering desperately to get out of the slipstream – I think it had misjudged the height of the lorry. It was all in slow motion – the bird hit the side of the lorry with a resounding thwack and bounced through the open car window, rapping me sharply on the shoulder. The poor dead falcon then very generously shared its entire complement of feathers with me: it obviously knew it didn't need them any more. It was like travelling in a particularly bad snowstorm in Siberia. I had been cautioned by the Establishment Section that I should not take animals in the office car, as they were so generous with their body coverings and their innards.

Why, oh why you might well ask, did I have the window open – wasn't it asking for trouble? It was, and it came. I eyed the feathers of the falcon that were liberally strewn round the car with some trepidation – it took an hour to vacuum clean the car out, and there were still feathers hidden in unlikely places.

I left the falcon on the floor to prove my story and, provokingly, was warned by the Establishments Section that birds should not be allowed into the car – surely I could have assumed as much as they did not allow goats and dogs in either. I was a little hurt at this sharp rebuke – it really wasn't my fault a goat had got into the boot of the car whilst I was collecting some important archives from a museum. By the time I returned to the car, staggering under a huge box of drawings and plans, it had eaten chunks out of the upholstery, evacuated its bowels and strewn a liberal amount of its hair throughout. It also bit me hard on the bottom as I was trying to get it out. I was hard put to see the funny side then, but I wonder if it was maybe incidents such as these that gave me the incentive to develop the protection technique I teach for cars, houses and personal property, as well as for people. I think on some level I had already begun to develop these techniques, as none of the archives I transported ever suffered the damage and degradation I and my family and my surroundings did.

Disasters flocked like hungry vampires to ensure complacency and boredom did not feature large in my life. One of the most memorable occasions – the subject of another documentary – was when a heron dropped a large pike on my sun roof, cracking it. I had watched the heron flying towards me from the ponds on my left on the M4 and noted with some apprehension that it was the biggest fish I had ever seen in my life, and that it was wriggling vigorously in the heron's claws. Foolishly, perhaps, I accelerated – in order to be out of the flight path. The heron veered dramatically to the left and, as it passed overhead, dropped the pike.

The fish skidded across the sun roof and bounced in front of a large lorry overtaking me in the middle lane. The lorry driver could not avoid squashing it. As I pulled onto the hard shoulder, the lorry pulled in behind me, and as I got out to check the sun roof the lorry driver jumped down and came to join me. He was shaking with laughter, and as he wiped his eyes he said to me, "I guess it weren't that pike's day to day, was it... there 'e was, having his breakfast when he gets tweaked out of the water. He only just gets used to flying when he falls on his 'ead and then gets squashed." I have to say, it was one of the occasions when my humour seemed to have gone on holiday, and with a brief smile I returned to the driving seat and left. It was after all my own car that was damaged this time. Needless to say, everyone at work thought it very funny indeed.

My car became the focus of many other major – and minor problems. Obviously my daily travels to and from Swindon stacked up the odds slightly, but others manage it without problems, so why should I be different (said with a definite whine)? I was travelling down, as usual, on the M4 when with a mighty clang my silencer fell off. It was only seven in the morning, with few cars around, so I pulled on to the hard shoulder and leapt nimbly out of the car, stowing the silencer quickly into the boot. I had only gone a couple of miles, wishing I had ear mufflers, when a police car pulled me over.

A large and rather serious looking policeman strolled over to the car. "Tell me, madam," he said politely, "is it against your religious convictions to have a silencer?" He looked at me stonily as I tried hard not to have hysterics – I'm not sure he even meant to be funny! I started to tell him that it had only just fallen off and.... He held up a hand.

"Madam," he said, "I do so hope you were not going to tell me you got out of the car and picked it up... that is illegal".

I hastily shut my mouth. The policeman kindly gave me an escort to my garage in Newbury, explaining that this might prevent me being murdered by all the other people I came across on the way.

We have bought all our cars from the garage, and once we had safely arrived I was lent a car for the day. I carefully rang up my insurance company and told them the new number of the car. I had proceeded approximately half a mile down the road when the fan belt packed up. I rang the insurance company again to tell them that I was now going to be driving a different car for the day.

The Skoda looked quite happy to see me... I climbed in and proceeded uneventfully to Swindon. I think the day proceeded smoothly – or what passes for smoothly with me. That night, when I came out, the battery was flat, and the steering wheel locked. Eventually, the entire staff from the security desk managed to get me started, and I left in a cloud of smoke. I was travelling merrily along when I arrived at a traffic jam outside Newbury. This seemed to be the cue the Skoda had been waiting for: after only two minutes of waiting, there was a loud bang followed by a cloud of smoke from the front of the car that could have been used to send smoke signals to Australia.

Anxiously I left the car, as did several motorists next to me. One hardy soul opened the front and looked in. "Oh, phew," he said, "the engine is in the back – your radiator has burst, that's all".

I rang my garage, again and explained the problem. The AA patrol arrived very quickly (he was less friendly later in the day) and towed me back to the garage. I picked up my car, apologising – as usual – for all the problems. I was so pleased to see my faithful Peugeot 309 – my stalwart helper that so rarely let me down. I had hardly reached the M4 again, when I had a puncture. I pulled on to the hard shoulder and waited for the AA. A police car pulled in front of me and the same policeman got out and crossed to me. For a moment, he was speechless.

"You again," he said in ringing tones. "Can you tell me when you are coming this way again so that I can be off duty?" A little harsh, I felt, as I had only seen him three times that day. Yes, he looked after me whilst I was waiting for the AA to come to the burst radiator.

The accidents seemed to calm down after that and I settled down to my daily journey with a reasonable – for me – number of punctures and broken windscreens. Just prior to leaving my heritage job in 1996, however, a significant event took place that I only fully appreciated after I had increased my knowledge and competence greatly in psychic matters.

Once a week visiting speakers came to give lectures in the lunch hour. One of these lectures was given by the Chairman of the Military Ridgeways and Aviation Authority. He had an enormous collection of aerial photographs and slides of military sites and airfields from the war. He was a good speaker, but I found myself, as usually, going to sleep as he showed lots of significant slides. I was a good three parts asleep when I felt as if I had been shaken hard by the shoulder. The Chairman was clearing his throat in an embarrassed way.

"I want to show you this sequence of slides – just because it's so strange and will wake up those of you who are going to sleep." This, addressed accusingly to me. The first slide was of a large field covered in tarmac and with a huge white cross painted across the middle of it. It looked like something rather naff out of an Ealing Studios film.

The chairman looked rather embarrassed as he admitted to being defeated by the significance of this field, but said that every night for four years the Germans had bombed it to smithereens. Each morning there had been frantic activity to get enough soil and rubble to fill the crater, repair the tarmac and paint the white cross on again, ready for the next night's bombing. The final aerial photograph taken in 1944 showed a convoy of tipper trucks making their way to the 'airfield' carrying what looked like iron bedsteads, old sofas, doors, carpets etc... the locals must by this time have reached rock bottom for 'hole fillers'. At the end of the war, there was a 150-foot deep crater in the field.

The chairman pointed out how extremely lucky this activity had been for the English, as close by were five airfields where different parts of the planes were manufactured, transported and then assembled. They had, on the whole, been unscathed. I felt a flock of ghostly mice run up and down my back (well, I had experienced a real live squirrel fall down my back and it felt like that). I knew, seriously, that this was a most significant fact I had been given. I wracked my brains for weeks when I thought about it, but could make no sense.

It was only when speaking to my mother shortly before her death that an explanation was given me and opened my eyes to endless possibilities. I was aware that both she and my father had worked for the RAF/Secret Service during the war – after all, it was from Mum that I inherited my love of motorbikes, although I would not fancy taking despatches by bike in the dead of night, with a slit of headlight showing, from Whitehall to the Basingstoke ferry. I have been unable to find out anything about this mysterious 'post' that my mum visited twice a week for a year: after she had delivered the despatches, they were taken on to another location. All that she would say was that it was from there that she often communicated telepathically with my dad.

In between rushing about Germany and France, my father was based at RAF Melksham. My mum knew he had developed a technique for transmitting 'mind pictures' that could and would be received by the target viewers: these were enemy planes flying overhead. There are of course several aspects to this – the picture itself, the transmission and the reception of the information. My dad also had to establish – to use a common computer term – a data audit trail, to show the progressive disintegration of the dummy airfield as bombs fell on it and destroyed it. These pictures were somehow focused on the white cross and a picture was built up of a busy airfield complete with planes waiting to take off. My father then trained officers also to transmit these mind pictures. Oh, how I wish I had learnt to do that.

When I talked with a good friend of mine about these activities she was gob smacked. She read this chapter and squeaked, "You cannot put it in as a throw-away line that something as revolutionary as psychic projection took place in the Second World War and no one knew anything about it!" Presumably, the powers-that-be knew about it – after all, it did help the war effort.

I suspect that over the next two or three decades such activities are going to become commonplace, and hope that this book will play a part in this constructive change to our thinking.

I left my job, finally. The staff gave me the most amazing A2 farewell card presenting a pictorial record of some of my exploits whilst employed there. The duck and the heron were there, as indeed were the incidents with the laminator, the snake in the deeds box, the collapse of the stage whilst I was giving my very serious talk at the art college, and of course when an entire section of large red boxes fell at Virginia Bottomley's feet. Such an eventful life! And I couldn't help but think that a lot of the people who had signed my card must have been breathing a secret sigh of relief to see me go at last. When I return occasionally, I can hear the sentries on the battlements warning of my arrival. So far they haven't poured any boiling oil on my head or shot fiery arrows at me. They were happy days indeed!

Chapter 5

PSYCHIC MISHAPS AND DEVELOPMENTS

THE FAREWELL CARD BROUGHT HOME to me again that I was really not particularly normal - that most people live uneventful lives unless they intersect with me. So, just after my departure from my heritage job, I decided to try and do something about my clumsiness and accident-prone career and investigate and identify 'psychic power'. I thought I would open the door to knowledge a little, so that I could peer round it. Within seconds, I was hanging on for dear life as a blast of information and power nearly blew me off my feet. I was about to enter into a world that I had suspected existed, but did not really believe in.

The part of my brain I had never intentionally used before kicked in with a vengeance, and hidden powers and abilities nearly overwhelmed me with sensory overload. The quest was on to find a master to follow like a little lamb and trot meekly down the path to psychicdom. What I found was a great number of charlatans that can trap and frighten the psychic in the early growth days; there is also a great number of deluded people who will go to elaborate lengths to decry and mock an ability they do not have access to themselves.

I had heard that it was possible to use crystals to heal and open the mind (even more), so I visited a crystal healer in Notting Hill Gate - one of the most delightful and pure people I have ever met. She lived in a flat, surrounded by crystals of every shape and size. At that point I was not yet Conan, the Great Destroyer of Innocent Crystals - that followed later. I talked with her for a bit about my eventful life, then she told me to lie down on a couch (also surrounded by crystals). I felt incredibly safe with her, and as she promised me that nothing could harm me, that I could relax and learn about myself, I let down my defences. Slowly she passed her hands over the space around my body. Suddenly I was aware that some part of me was standing in a room in front of three men who were involved in some dark and dangerous magic. Even more weird, they could see me! I'm not sure who was the most surprised - me or them!

I knew the house was in Norwich, and asked Anne if she knew these men. She went quite pale, but before she could speak I was at a ritual being carried out in an Egyptian temple. The man who was carrying out the ritual was tall and fair, and his name was David. I returned quickly to the couch, severely shaken. How on earth had I gone walkabout when I was supposed to be protected?

Anne was very shaken too – she confirmed that her boyfriend was an Egyptian priest, and that he had got involved in a black magic circle centred in Norwich. I left her soon after that, feeling most uneasy. I had just got onto my motorbike when I started to feel desperately cold, and then feverishly hot. By the time I got home I couldn't even stand, and collapsed against our front door. Fortunately, my husband heard the crash and helped me to bed. By this time I had a temperature of 103° and could hardly breathe. He called the doctor, who arrived very quickly. After seeing me, he gravely shook his head, "Why didn't you call me before, she has double pneumonia?"

He then arranged for me to be admitted to hospital. By the time the ambulance came, I was throwing up and had all the symptoms of dysentery: my temperature was normal. I returned, weak and shaking, to bed. The worst headache I have ever had then hit me like a ton of bricks. I was unable to bend my head and a rash had appeared all over my chest. This lasted about two hours, then finally my joints stiffened up and swelled so badly that I was unable to raise myself up on bed.

Twelve hours after I had visited Anne, I was better, but pretty angry. I have to admit that I did not moderate my language when I told her about my various illnesses and ailments. I knew, with absolute certainty, that it was connected with my visit to her.

"It shouldn't have happened," she said sadly. "But yes, over the last two days before I saw you I had patients with pneumonia, dysentery, viral meningitis and acute osteo-arthritis".

This is a cautionary tale; I should have noticed that in the corner of her room stood a guardian crystal that was too big to be washed.

As most people are aware, crystals transmit and store information: washing and cleansing them thoroughly to remove the 'charge' is vital. Anne had washed the smaller crystals but the huge crystal carried a faithful recording of events during healing. Again, I learnt a lesson, but not the one I hoped to! I was still not fully aware of my abilities and how on earth to develop them.

Life in the Fast Lane – or the Hard Shoulder

As I have already mentioned, I decided to grasp the nettle and investigate the nature of the viper I was harbouring in my breast (this is exactly how I felt as I looked cautiously at what I could do by mistake) and attended my first 'psychic' course in the summer. It was a glorious summer that year, and I was greatly looking forward to my first course on Intuition. The course took place in a local community hall and was run by a gracious and attractive ex-GP. She had, she told us, left general practise when she realised that the mind and spirit were not being looked after adequately by conventional medicine. She was, and is, an extremely powerful lady, elegantly dressed, fluent and convincing. She is renowned in England and America and is the writer of many books.

The other students, a variety of people with a predominance

of women, were a mixed bunch. The sun shone warmly into the room, making us all slightly drowsy, and the women in their bright cotton dresses looked like resting butterflies as they gently fanned themselves with their notebooks. I was aware of a feeling of amused detachment as I looked round the room; I noticed the earnest young man with runaway glasses and a nervous tic, the solicitor who was there to accompany his exotic wife, and my husband and I, the onlookers.

The course proceeded smoothly. The speaker spoke at length about intuition - that sixth sense that we all apparently have, that warns and guides us if we will but listen to it. She spoke of progression - of fine-tuning this innate ability in our everyday lives, and then gave us exercises to prove its existence. I became uncomfortably aware, as the day progressed, that my intuition was either non-existent or had gone on holiday. I was beginning to search frantically for excuses to leave whilst I still had some self-respect left when we broke for lunch. Everyone vanished into the large grounds and spattered themselves out beneath the very hot sun. As a burner, I stayed inside with the last two people in the room.

I became aware that they were staring fixedly at the top of my head. I wondered if I had twigs in my hair, or more likely, that at last my saintly personality was manifesting itself as a halo of gold round my sacred head. Finally, they broke the somewhat tense silence. "Its your aura," they breathed reverently. I can honestly say that until that moment I had never even heard of a 'Roarer' and was surprised I had one. I do know now of course!

"Ahhhh," I breathed knowledgeably, and waited. To my astonishment, they smiled at me vaguely and left the room. Shaking my head sadly, I settled down with a good book.

"You'll be working with me in the next exercise, I'm Leah." The girl who had spoken to me had a mobile, intelligent face, and I wondered what on earth she was doing with all us nuts (I had by now included myself in that category - after all, I had a 'Roarer'). I was flattered that such a normal looking person should want to work with me, and thanked her. She looked at me strangely for a moment, then told me that it wasn't her choice, she had been told by her guides that this was so.

I have to say that by now I had passed the stage of stupefaction and was thoroughly enjoying myself. When all the rest of the class returned to their chairs, I smiled benignly at them and waited for the next exercise. This one was quite different - the speaker divided the class into teams of three people. One member of the team at a time was asked to 'pose' as for a portrait painting, whilst the other two members studied and made notes about the sitter. We were told to write down everything that came into our minds, whether seemingly relevant or not: I was assigned to Leah, of course, and an elderly Polish Jew who was the first subject. I was fascinated to realise how much information we all present to the world by our clothes, posture and faces. I was busy making notes, absorbed by this exercise in psychology, when I suddenly realised that I also knew that our subject, the Jewish gentleman, was a widower, that his only son was dying of cancer and that I could describe where he lived. The pain I felt for that gentle man is indescribable. The vivid pictures sounds and colours that flooded my mind overwhelmed me. I was on sensory overload.

Fortunately (or perhaps using her intuition), our team leader suddenly appeared beside me, crouched down and told me, rather curtly, that she could spare me two minutes and no more, but that she had a message for me. The message she gave me was a turning point of my life. She said, baldly, that I had been chosen for a unique mission for mankind, that I was a psychic and healer and that I would be renowned and respected as a teacher and lecturer throughout the world. She also told me that I would find no path to follow; I was to hack my own way through the undergrowth of life. I think, with the wisdom of hindsight, that I should have paid more attention to that tough and lonely analogy. I hope that most emerging psychics have a gentler 'birthing'; to say I was stunned is an understatement. I was gobsmacked. I would probably have dismissed the whole thing with some humour, a lot of pity and a feeling of peevishness about having wasted the day with some nut. However, just after my fateful meeting with my erstwhile GP, and whilst I was still fairly shell-shocked, I met another powerful lady. Being the owner of four dogs makes a walk on the common a constitutional necessity. It is a beautiful common in all seasons, with little to disturb the thoughts of the walker apart from the occasional polite asides to fellow dog walkers, and sometimes detaching the dog's teeth from the throat of another for some imagined affront. It was with great astonishment that I realised that I was being hailed by the epitome of gypsiness.

I had heard of the power of the true Romany, but nothing had prepared me for the reality. I was completely transfixed, like a rabbit before a snake. She was tall, about six feet, with a regal bearing, flashing brown eyes and black hair. She was dressed in traditional gypsy dress, with golden bangles that tinkled as she moved her arms. She stopped in front of me in silence. I cleared my throat nervously, and explained that I had no money with me on the common, and would much rather she didn't curse me because of this. She smiled grimly, and then stared deeply into my eyes again. She said payment must be made, but that she knew I had just been made redundant and that times were hard. All she was asking me was that I would look after one of her own if I saw them in trouble. This I readily agreed to do.

Taking my shoulders with both hands, she then repeated the message of fame and fortune that had been given me the week before. She gave me an old Romany blessing, removed her hands, tossed her hair and walked briskly away. I was a little disappointed, I had expected her to vanish into thin air, or, even better, take to her broomstick.

I was at this point still waiting for fame and fortune to fall like ripe plums into my expectant lap: I didn't realise then that life really isn't like that, and that I would have probably squashed the plums anyway by careless handling.

Forwards, Always Forwards

I did not realise, in fact, that I was now well and truly launched on my psychic journey - rather like the magician's apprentice, I continued to create havoc wherever I went. I saw a huge number of clairvoyants and psychics who I hoped would help me sort out my future. With few exceptions, they all told me that I had great powers, but I had to learn to ground myself. This was the first time I had come up against the term, and I asked all and sundry how I could do it. I had, apparently, to somehow make myself part of the earth, so that I was firmly rooted instead of floating a foot or so above it (Oh boy, I wish, I would be a millionaire at least if that were true!) Several pictures came to mind – for example, lying in a big trench with my saintly hands folded demurely on my chest, or perhaps going to a power station and grabbing the earthing wire on the big generator (Lucky I didn't try that one, or this book would not have been written!)

My poor long-suffering husband looked at me rather worriedly as I tried to find my own solution. I sat glumly in my chair at home with my feet in a bucket of cold water, visualising my 'roots' going into the ground. I placed a metal bowl on my head for insulation. I must have looked like a disgruntled oyster, and if I didn't look like it, I felt like one. I really did spend hours... all that I developed was a severe head cold blessed with sneezes that probably started an avalanche in Siberia and very wet and wrinkly feet. Another failure, I thought sadly – I remained 'unearthed', so the Holy Man in Amsterdam told me on my disastrous visit.

I realised how ignorant I was of even the basics of psychosity, and in order to try and understand what was going on I devoured every relevant book I could find. Snippets were useful, the total contents unhelpful. I searched for courses that would further my advancement but found few that I could see would be of use whilst I waited for famedom to raise me to the heights. I hoped that I might get a few more qualifications under my black belt.

My Judo exploits are not mentioned in great detail in this book, as frankly, they are rather boring! I didn't even break a rib, or anyone else's, during my training. The only memorable thing was that I had a chance to go with the Women's Olympic Team when this event was introduced, but whilst training I became pregnant with my son (well, not literally). Maybe I would have been queen of the psychic Judo circuits, if not for this.

I decided to experiment and learn on my own. I fell down every psychic hole and trap there was, stumbled over obstacles, and was generally very miserable for some time. I could find no one to help me for more than a few steps. It is all very well being told, as I had been, how wonderful and special you are, but how do you capitalise on all this talent? - I felt that I had grown a second head that had its own mind and I have to admit I had expected to smoothly sail down the psychic river in a gentle and learned way. This, fortunately, has not been my experience – development is very exciting!

When I was first developing, I remember clearly an incident with a very good friend of mine, Suzie. I had met her for coffee, and as we sat drinking I remarked casually that I was delighted that her sister Caroline was pregnant again. She nearly dropped her cup of coffee.

"How on earth did you know?" she gasped. "I only heard this morning".

I waved my hands about in a distracted fashion, efficiently decapitating most of the freesias in the vase.

"Must have been someone else," I mumbled.

Several weeks later I met her again for coffee. I patted her hand consolingly. "I'm so sorry about Caroline's baby – at least she didn't lose it later in her pregnancy."

Suzie looked at me in complete bewilderment. "Wrong person again," she said crossly. She literally stalked out of the café – I followed her after I had again mopped up the water from the vase and scooped the flower heads under my coffee cup, where hopefully they would not be noticed until I had left. By this time she was a dot on the horizon getting smaller by the second.

I had a phone call that night. It was Suzie.

"I have just heard from my sister – she had a miscarriage late last night."

I really did not know what to say to her - commiserate again for her sister, or leap up and down and be pleased that I had got it right? I think (in self-interest) I shall let you guess which route I followed!

Baby Psychic

At this point, I was behaving exactly as Father Shaw had feared – no self-discipline or indeed sensitivity. I had rather brutally told Suzy what I saw just to prove myself – I really was a spoilt and naughty 'baby psychic'.

What I most remember of those early days is the lure of psychic power... It is very exciting to realise that events, people and places can be manipulated just for the hell of it. It is rather like giving a toddler a stick of dynamite and some matches to hold. There is the strong possibility that, against all the odds, the toddler will manage to light the fuse... at which point it is wise for bystanders to run away rather quickly. Thinking about it, I wonder if that is why so many psychics have thin eyebrows – when they were baby psychics, they blew them off!

I found it very tempting to remain childish - give people headaches if they crossed me. And of course to fuse their lights. Once this stage of development has passed, it is almost impossible to do this. I think the power is rawer when it is undeveloped - it is perhaps like an aboriginal artist painting amazingly-alive native paintings. When art school is attended, that primitive feeling and colour is somehow lost.

In early growth days there seemed to be an enormous amount of power to play with – I am sometimes peeved that when I get very cross with someone I can no longer zap them: with the onset of psychic adolescence I developed psychic acne and had only a pathetic little whisper of my former power. It really is most disconcerting at one moment to be able to throw power like a javelin, straight and true, and the next to be throwing wilting celery. I can look back with some nostalgia to those days

It was just after I opened the floodgates, and whilst I was still a baby psychic, that I enlisted the help of 'the Sceptic' to help me write a book to help others have a smoother birthing and development. My co-author ran holistic massage classes at my local college, and is one of the steadiest people I have ever met. I don't actually think she quite realised what she was letting herself in for! She is determined and spirited... and rock-like in her reliability. She accepted nothing at face value – I had to justify every statement I made.

She has, with a great deal of humour, helped me to define my boundaries and made me see when I am being bad mannered and intruding on her space. It was from her that I learnt how to see the pictures people carry without the need to conduct an archaeological dig. Talking about how I had accessed all her memory banks very nearly brought about such a major bust up that, again, this book might not have been written. She has nagged, cajoled and encouraged me to become less splashy with my power and become steadier and more reliable with it.

It is hard to write a book when the picture is constantly changing - or as the different 'ages' of psychicness are reached. Indeed, one of the problems the Sceptic and I have faced is the elusiveness of capturing the thoughts, happenings and growth periods of psychic development before the 'magic' and the terror are somehow lost. It is important that the various growth spurts and the plateaus be charted, because although they will not be same for everyone, the pattern will remain constant.

The Sceptic has been battered and buffeted by my excitement as I try to capture what is going on; as she so wisely says, I do not realise how far I have developed since my first exploratory outings into uncharted territories. Psychic development was a thorny subject when this book was begun: we were aware of how controversial some of the ideas were. Now, with countless television and radio programmes dedicated to the 'alternative society', they are not. It is normal to be psychic, not paranormal. All members of the human race, I repeat, boringly, share my abilities.

The Sceptic and I have spent many happy hours dissecting and discussing learnedly how psychic power can be used - and abused! We decided to carry out experiments to see what would happen. Many happy and unproductive hours were spent in trying to move a matchstick across a bowl of water by will, and attempting to transfer information from mind to mind... all to no avail. Intense concentration on both resulted in very soggy matches, dizzy spells from over-eager breathing, and a cracking headache. Information transfer fared no better– I could just not say what playing card she was thinking of. It is interesting that although I was already accessing her mind on another level, somehow we felt we had to find a demonstrable, respectable formula.

I was a little depressed, on one level, that I was not able to control my abilities and use them immediately: I have often spoken to the Sceptic about the energy fields I could see around people and things – like a bat, I can sense where things are. I decided to experiment with this. I would like to add here, that surprisingly, no one has ever doubted that I can do what I say: maybe I hypnotise people into believing me. (I hope not.)

I was caught in a long traffic jam in Cromwell Road, London. I was in a bit of a hurry; all three lanes were stationary so I drove my motorbike down between the cars on the outside and those on the middle lane. I had for some time been aware that it is easier to sense where stationary objects – eg. mirrors - are when there is no visual distraction. I shut my eyes and used my mind to feel where cars and mirrors and so on were, and manoeuvred round them without conscious thought until I reached the traffic lights. A fellow biker drew in beside me – he had been travelling between the first and second lanes. He was a rather dashing young man, with a long thick pony tail, wildly painted leathers and a courier tabard.

"Blood 'ell", he said graphically. "Are you a courier? If not, don't even consider doing it, you're too damn fast." He was then gone in a belch of black smoke.

I had by this time spoken to a lot of people in my quest for knowledge, and just after this I was introduced to a Reiki Master who ran a healing and discussion group in Tunbridge Wells. He asked me if I would like to share my experiences as a 'baby psychic' and give a talk to his group – they met every Friday night over a homoeopathic chemist's shop.

I was a little nervous: this, after all, I was not a subject about which I had a great deal of experience – I was more used to talking to archivists and curators. The audience were all nice smiley people, however, who quickly put me at ease.

I spoke of all my mishaps – most of them had heard of my disasters through the group leader, Bob. After that, I passed on to the necessity of keeping a tight control over the mind's powers and the morality and responsibility of using these powers. I failed at first to see the look of consternation on their faces as I described my interference in other people's lives – using my will to intervene and interfere.

I told them of how I had intervened in a fight. I think they could understand the temptation to interfere in this instance. I had gone to a conference on business management and, as I came out of the hotel into the huge car park outside, I heard angry voices.

I crossed over to the darkest part of the car park, reluctantly, I have to say. Two men – an older one with a careworn face and a very smartly dressed young man – were confronting each other with wicked looking knives. With a resigned sigh, I addressed the older man. Because I could see the pictures both men carried in their heads, I could remind him that his wife and three children needed him, but that he was about to die if he took part in the fight. His knife was a long bladed extremely sharp butcher's knife, and he held it purposefully.

The other man was about nineteen, and high on drugs. His knife was a stiletto. I clearly saw two futures for him. One of the areas that fascinate me is how the future works – it seems to be more flexible than we think: was I written into the script of the men's lives, or did I interrupt their Karma with my help? I really don't know, but probably will when I eventually die!

I told the young man that if he had this fight, he would win, but in a separate incident he would be killed and his body would be found face down in a canal. I reminded him of how much his mother loved him, and that she lit a candle for him every day in church. I also told him that the man he was fighting had indeed spent all their ill-gotten gains from a robbery, but that it had been used to obtain hospital treatment for his daughter in America.

There was a stunned silence as the two men looked at me with their mouths open (looking rather like landed trout). Then with one accord, they looked at each other, then again at me in disgust. "These nutters shouldn't be allowed out," said the older man.

"I agree," said the younger. "They're a menace to society."

Without another word they walked off in opposite directions, leaving me wanting to howl like an orphaned alligator.

I told the group that I had read a book about the CIA and the gross misuse of the power, and felt very noble about using my power well and for the good of mankind, to quote a cliché. Then I had fallen from grace with a mighty crash that must have caused an earthquake in the Outer Hebrides. Quite deliberately I had acted like a spoilt and malicious child and sent resentful thoughts to two of my friends for not coming to my housewarming party. One had an inexplicable car crash that night and wrote off his van completely, and the other had a burst appendix in the early hours of the following morning.

I spoke of the several experiments I had carried out that had damaged both my motorbike and me! I had been thinking hard about my dad's interaction with the wing of the Valiant and decided to see if I could affect the brakes on my bike. Really, what a twit. I was travelling down the A4 as I thought about the brake disks, and saw them disconnected in some way from the bike. The van in front of me stopped suddenly, I didn't. I bounced off the back of the van and landed in a tangled heap on the road. When, eventually, my poor bike was taken to the garage for repair, the mechanic remarked that he didn't understand how my brakes had broken down into their component parts and were not connected to each other in any way. Needless to say, I did not enlighten him, although I was aware of having a face as red as a Hawaiian sunset.

I hesitated for a moment – should I confess to the group that one of the truly sad things about this story was that I didn't learn from my experience and carried out another experiment in a similar vein, again causing disaster? I decided that I would tell them, as the second incident was in some ways rather humorous. I had become aware that everything and everybody has an 'electrical' energy field round them, and whilst travelling down Cromwell Road – again on my bike – I had decided to see if I could shut down the energy field of the bike. As I was thinking this, I arrived at the traffic lights. The lights turned green and I continued on. The taxi on my outside however didn't continue straight on – he turned left, sweeping my bike and I round the corner with him. I slid gracefully – like a greased hippopotamus – across his bonnet, and my bike bounced its cheerful way down the road without me. My main feeling was of acute embarrassment – how could I have been so stupid?

I spoke to the taxi driver, who was rather incoherently swearing that I must have appeared out of nowhere, he hadn't seen me. I hobbled away from him and started to organise someone to help me lift my bike off the road so that the traffic could continue to flow smoothly, and then hobbled back to some nearby steps and sat down rubbing my bruised leg.

As I sat there, deciding that I could proceed after all, that my leg was not shattered into a million fragments (after all, I was the expert on breakages of every kind), a policeman on a motorbike arrived. I looked at him blankly as he rushed about, asking in a loud voice where the critically injured biker was. I held my hand up timidly as a police car with a doctor inside arrived. Both converged on me, their expressions worried. I explained to them that I really was not hurt – it was just a bruise on my leg – when the ambulance arrived. Then, to cap the icing on the snowplough or whatever the expression is, an accident emergency helicopter arrived on the scene. By this time I wished the pavement had opened and that I had been swallowed up.

As I looked at the sea of faces round me, I asked rather plaintively if I could show my glorious war wounds to everyone at once, and explained that I hadn't phoned them, that I wasn't deliberately wasting anybody's time, and that I was very sorry to have bothered them. I had visions of being charged a fortune!

The helicopter only hovered for a minute or two, thank goodness. As I watched all the terribly smart city gents desperately trying to keep their bowler hats on, the children in push chairs holding onto their precious toys and blankets to prevent them being blown to Spain and the passers-by holding on for dear life to their possessions as the terrific updraft from the helicopter blades whisked round them, I was mortified.

I became aware that the policeman on the motorbike – who had become quite a good friend in all this – kept on hurrying over to his bike and burying his face in the back box. I thought it was some obscure religious ritual and that maybe he was a Freemason or something, but then I realised it was because he was desperately trying not to show me how funny he thought the whole thing was. Well, if you are going to do something disastrous, do it well, say I. I think the Tunbridge Wells group coped with me admirably, to their great credit. When I finished my talk, they spoke to me with words of love and sympathy – but also of bewilderment. Over and over again, they expressed amazement that these things were possible with the mind – surely my problems were of a spiritual nature, and that guys from other dimensions were interacting with me in a destructive way. For once, I was silenced!

Psychic Adolescence

So I had cut my teeth, learnt to walk and talk and become a stroppy adolescent. I remember clearly one morning, whilst resentfully cleaning out a room, that I threw an ashtray out of the door, commanding it to go into the cardboard box at the end of the long corridor. The metal ashtray coasted gracefully along until it was about two feet from the box. It then fell on the carpet, bounced up onto the wall, slid along the wall, hit the upstanding flap at the back of the box and landed gracefully in the exact middle of the box. I was most impressed, but also rather bewildered. How perverse, it would have been easier to just throw it into the box. Time and again there is an easy way to achieve things but it is the harder way that succeeds. I was, and indeed am (still) occasionally, plagued with long days of self-doubt, followed by hours (one or two if I'm lucky) of knowing that I am indeed powerful and wonderful and a joy to behold.

I was roaring down the adolescent highway when I started to interfere with my electrical surroundings on a larger scale. I had gone to a recording studio to make a relaxation tape: I am amazed we succeeded. As I began to read my bit in measured tones, all the sound systems equipment packed up - including their editing suite. Fortunately the two engineers did not at this point connect it with my presence, although I did look rather guilty. I really don't know why I tried to sabotage my recordings – very strange. Finally, we sorted out the problems, and I recorded my tape again. I left soon after that.

The following day I had a phone call from one of the engineers - he asked me if I was a witch doctor or something. When they checked the recording they had made, the tape blanked itself as they listened. I expressed untold astonishment, but on my second visit it was thought prudent that I sat outside the studio and recorded remotely.

There was still the minor problem of no music in the background of the tape, although I was speaking over a soothing and extremely banal tune. I left, whilst they were still tearing their hair out in handfuls. Afterwards, they were able, with great difficulty, to eliminate the repeated phrases that had suddenly appeared, the ghostly gongs, and improve the sound quality to an acceptable level.

Needless perhaps to say, they did not suggest I made a follow-up tape: I had tentatively at the beginning mentioned the possibility of making a series to accompany my workshops. In fact, in insulting haste, they dived for their book of recording studios and recommended one or two to me. I think that this may have not been very ethical, as they spoke in undertones about which studio had undercut them for a contract, and which one deserved my presence the most. Eventually I left, with the dreadful feeling that I was seen as a nemesis for recording studios – that my presence was not conducive to a smooth running operation.

One of the reasons why I decided to write this book, as I have already mentioned, is that I had been unable to find a book or teacher to help me to progress in a less erratic fashion. I had always interacted to some extent destructively with my environment - like a mini-tornado, but once I had unleashed and accessed my power it was almost uncontrollable and my co-author, the Sceptic, got caught up in the maelstrom of my emerging abilities.

Having survived (somehow) psychic babyhood, I could see that the rewards for good behaviour and the sharp raps on the knuckles for self-pity and tantrums had borne good fruit... Somehow the Sceptic understood that I felt as if I had grown a second independent head – typical adolescent feelings!

To try and control my 'psychic hormones' and understand what was going on I looked for relevant courses that could be useful and just after we started writing this book, I attended a course on Herbal medicine not entirely related, but useful. The course is an accredited one, from which a diploma can be gained. Aha, respectability at last, thought I!

The course is an extremely effective introduction to herbalism and the use of plants in every aspect of our lives. In order to gain accreditation, there is homework and compulsory attendance on several weekend courses during which lectures and workshops take place. This course gave me great insight into the whole field of complementary medicine – the theory, practice and practitioners!

The tutor, an extremely able and well-qualified medical herbalist, gave fascinating talks about the properties of plants. The class consisted of about thirty people, sitting in a circle of desks. We passed round the various plants she was talking about. When they reached me, I nearly dropped them! I could say what they were for, if I was allergic to them, and rather surprisingly, I could see pictures and feel the emotions of the people involved in their preparation. I had of course already experienced this aspect of psychometry when I had lain on Anne-the-crystal-healer's couch. This time it was stronger. As I have said before, as you begin to use your abilities you will bounce from strength to strength.

As I had only just stopped being a baby psychic, when I was asked for my opinion about the plants I blurted out a jumble of facts and information. The tutor looked at me rather blankly then asked me to speak to her afterwards. My fellow pupils were frankly a little surprised. It was, interestingly enough, at these weekends that my psychic development in many areas accelerated dramatically. The tutor, a beautifully turned out and elegant blond, continued to find me startling throughout the course. Please, fellow psychics, try to avoid the trap of trying to prove yourself to others – both for your own sake and for theirs. In a desperate bid for respectability – or at least acknowledgment – I gave her lots of helpful information about her family. This was of course unsolicited – again, an unwarranted intrusion into someone's private life. She avoided me whenever possible for the rest of the course.

I found the weekends a treasure house of goodies – I learnt to smash crystals for the first time, use telekinesis violently and uncontrollably, walk about in people's minds and influence the progression of the teaching. The crystal smashing is still a great source of sadness to me: as we queued for our incredibly healthy (and I must say, delicious) lunch, I started to talk to a lovely girl – delicate as porcelain - who had her own shop selling psychic goodies, among them a fine collection of crystals and rocks. Her mistake, I think, was to show me the pouch of her most favourite clear quartz. She held them to me trustingly in her hand. I pounced on them with glee, avidly studying their innards and what made them work. I noticed they had lost a lot of their lustre whilst I was looking at them, but later on at lunch, she showed them to me, her eyes filled with tears. They were in splinters. I was so very sorry I had done that, but continue still to do this, despite my best resolutions.

Whilst writing this book and congratulating myself on having moved past this rather nasty and difficult stage and still retaining some psychic friends (and my good friend the Sceptic!), I attended a psychic fair in Wales and bought a fine collection of coloured quartz polished stones. I greatly admired all the colours, and brought some of them out of their bag because they were so beautiful. By the end of three hours, the inside was crazed – as if someone had taken a large hammer from the inside and was trying to smash their way out. Two weeks later, the cracks had reached the polished surface, and then the stones collapsed in on themselves. I had put two stones in a separate bag as a present, and it was with great trepidation that I peered into it. They were completely undamaged and went to their new home with a sigh of relief - from both sides.

I met one of my greatest buddies on this herbal course; we led each other astray – I think actually she led me astray – and we vanished as often as possible to the pub opposite. On one occasion we joined in on a musical 'pop' quiz. We should have won, but despite my psychic cheating and mind reading, an 85-year local won hands down. Ah, well.

The course also had a practical and spiritual approach – we went out plant gathering and harvesting, and we also learnt about Kundalini energy and its uses. I don't actually think that I could have survived the pace if we hadn't crept out between the practical part and the spiritual meditation and bought some fish and chips. The thing that surprised me was that although we had selected a shop miles from the village, at least four people reported seeing us indulging in hefty portions. Sneaks, eh?

When we returned from the pub to the room in the village hall, the stage area had been unveiled and most of the other people were already sitting cross-legged in an attitude of patience and peacefulness. Although I liked the leaders of the course, I was suddenly filled with foreboding. We sat down on the floor. The leader of the meditation was an amazingly attractive man who had trained in Tibet for fourteen years. He was a stunning mix of sexuality and spirituality: tall, dark and stormy eyed. We sat in silence whilst the leader explained what the meditation was about. The purpose was to raise the Kundalini energy that is dormant in us all. Through music and dancing, the energy would be raised from the base chakra through each of the other chakras until the crown chakra was reached, then taken down again into the earth.

I have to admit here that I really don't know very much about chakras, but if you want to find out more, there are many books written on the subject. However, a brief description of Kundalini energy can be found at the end of this book. The organiser explained that the music he had selected would serve as the channel for all this energy. I must admit I was at first rather tickled at the thought of grown men and women leaping about like demented dervishes in the semi-dark, with their eyes closed and grunting and moaning. Perhaps it was my sense of the ridiculous that prevented me from taking action. Then the humour left and I was aware of the power we were planning to raise and release. It was waiting like a tiger.

As the meditation proceeded, the power we were summoning appeared to me like a tornado rising from the floor. It was seductively attractive and promised fame, power, money and control. Afterwards I learned of the many organisations that deal with 'Kundalini crisis' for those individuals who have been overloaded with the power and to some extent been burnt out. The promise of all these goodies was almost too much for the poor psychic, to be recognised as a wonderful and special, and to have lots of pennies. Nobly, I resisted.

I left the stage, sick and trembling. Shortly after this, as the meditation was finished, I realised that it was rather cold so I shut the windows all round the room with a swift thought. I can occasionally do this, but on the whole it is easier to shut the windows the more conventional way. I suspect in fact that I wouldn't have even realised that I had done this if I hadn't been coldly reprimanded for being irresponsible and nearly catching someone's hand. The adolescent psychic had yet again had her wrists slapped for fiddling, but I was nevertheless rather proud of myself and got quite remarkably drunk in the pub.

All psychic ability seems to be accessed 'sideways', by concentrating your mind on the action rather than the purpose (I could shut the windows for fun, but had I tried harder I suspect I wouldn't have been able to). I think probably the rational part of us creeps in and says 'this isn't possible'. This is borne out by my experience with the Sceptic when we tried to move the matchsticks round in a bowl of water - it didn't work!

On the following day of the course, another meditation took place. Instead of just not going to this (probably because I had a fairly major hangover), which was the sensible thing to do, I took my place again and the fear returned, without the humour. In exasperation, the leader asked me to stop screwing the tapes up and turning off the tape player. He suggested I leave the room. This sort of psychic meddling has been repeated at regular intervals. Although (funnily enough) I could interfere with electrical appliances with ease, now that I am a psychic matron I find it very difficult.

During the last weekend prior to qualification, I was tremendously privileged to be allowed on a ritual harvesting expedition of various useful plants. I suspect that if my unfortunate sense of humour had again not led to my downfall, I would be a wiser woman than I am!

The harvesting took place under a full moon in a beautiful pastured field. There were numerous plants covered with the sheen of dew and the gossamer threads of spider's webs – the whole field glistened. The leader of the expedition – a serious young man with a pony tail and a spiritual face – asked us to form a circle round him. He handed us each some cotton and a small harvesting bag. As we stood in silence, heads bowed, he summoned the spirits of the plants we would be selecting and asked permission to harvest them. The somewhat irreverent thought crossed my mind that I didn't see how they could refuse even if they wanted to. After a further silence, he explained that we should pick our victims and place a piece of cotton loosely round the heads: he showed us some of the plants he had already selected. Despite the eerie beauty of the scene, I became aware that a bubble of laughter was forming under my appendix (or where it used to be), that my feet were decidedly damp and that a very large sneeze was working its way from my toenails.

I stood motionless, hoping that the nice young man would hurry up with his prayers of blessing prior to the slaughter. He didn't, and the sneeze erupted and echoed round the field, down the hill and probably into the nearby village: sorrowfully, he looked at me, as another sneeze wracked my body. Without a word, he went round the field taking the cotton off all his plants. I had broken the spell apparently – the show was over. I would swear, incidentally, that I heard the plants sigh with relief – probably caused by watching too many children's programmes like Bill and Ben, flower pot men.

Surprisingly enough, I was not asked to go on the next expedition, and in fact, when I recently told some of my pagan friends the story, they hastily withdrew their invitation to their waking the trees ceremony. There is a difference, they told me severely, between waking the trees gently with song and frightening them out of their collective wits.

Tunbridge Wells Revisited

It was towards the end of the adolescent stage that my friends in Tunbridge Wells asked me back to give a follow-on talk, now that I had matured a little. I returned to the same location, and almost the same people were present. I mentioned the herbal course, and one of the audience held up her hand rather timidly. She was a serene lady, obviously well in control of her Karma and her life, I thought enviously. I was sure she slept well, and if she didn't, I bet she didn't see how many stars she could make 'shoot', unlike – me. If the number of stars seems to be diminishing I will stop, honestly.

I realised I had missed the question, and asked her to repeat it.

"Have you become more responsible and less interactive with your environment?", she asked me, with a smile. I thought about it for a moment.

"Er, no", I told her, honestly. I then asked her to let me tell the story in my own way.

I told them of all the problems I was still having with lack of self-control, that I was really still as splashy in many ways as I had been before. I told them of the memorable occasion when my husband and I visited our local supermarket; I was extremely peeved that I couldn't get out of the car very easily, as the next one had parked too close. I flung the door open to get out. When my husband tried to shut the door he couldn't – the door had gone past the fixed mirror of the other car and it was impossible to close our door. Whilst he was still scratching his head in perplexity, the owner of the other car returned. They both looked at the problem. Then without another word the driver got into his car and left, giving me a deeply suspicious look, making 'warding of the evil eye' signs as he left.

I explained to the group that the interference with my electrical surroundings had intensified – I mentioned my experience with the music and lights during the Kundalini meditations and that, unfortunately, I was now beginning to have serious problems with my computer. Apart from wiping files regularly by looking at them, I had also begun to influence the calendar and clock. I had been convinced it was the 19th June, but in fact it was the 18th. Each time I thought it was the 19th, the computer clock changed and I had to change it back manually. I didn't mention that the year had also changed to 5,000 which, according to my helpful computer repairers, is not possible, as they told me while desperately trying to resolve the problem.

I had taken this interference problem to a good clairvoyant friend of mine who has given me a lot of support and care. I was thinking about the clock when I was sitting opposite her. As part of her readings, Jan shuffles tarot cards and gives the date of the reading. I suddenly realised she was saying the 8th of July, when in fact it was the 9th. I mentioned this to her diffidently and she started shuffling again, only to find the pattern repeated itself. It was only when I thought about other things that it sorted itself out! Fortunately, she was pleased with this unwarranted intrusion, as she said it showed how well I was doing.

I looked around the room at the silent and interested group, and reflected that perhaps I had come further than I thought - I had firmly taken control of 'accidental damage' to other's lives. I thought maybe I should leave my talk on this positive note, when one of the ladies at the far end of the circle help up her hand urgently.

"Can you help me, please. My family and I are under spiritual attack from our next door neighbour. All my children are ill with unknown, but serious illnesses. I won't pay him money to stop, as my other neighbours have." She then burst into floods of tears.

I was aware that the solution I was going to give her would mean that the group would once again look at me with either disgust or horror. I told them that I had recently had a succession of people coming to me for help – ex-boyfriends, con men, healers, and the like were damaging them seriously. I had devised a most interfering solution. I'm sure the Holy Man in

Amsterdam would have been so horrified that he would have predicted another two hundred and fifty four and a half more lives for me as an earthworm or a prickly pear: I'm not sure of the scoring system in Karmic terms, but I suspect it is accurate and mounts up quickly.

I crossed over to the woman, a small dark lady in her forties, and took her hands. Bother the rest of them, if they disapproved, then they disapproved. I could not withhold the help I knew I could give. I looked defiantly at the circle round me, but could only see a desperate compassion for the woman.

"I will place your neighbour in a plastic crystal", I told her. "He will be unable to send out bad thoughts to you, or to anyone else for that matter".

I explained that I had had amazing feedback from the other people I had helped. In each case within 24 hours of my intervention, damaged lives began to repair themselves. Actually, I had only just started to do this, and had not properly thought out the whole scenario. A person, deprived of the thoughts and feelings of those around him, will go sick. Now, when I do this, I place a 'computer' programme on the crystal that asks the 'prisoner' at regular intervals if they will now behave. If they agree, the crystal opens on its hinges. If they begin to damage people again, the crystal shuts once more. I have also placed a set of programmes on myself that will not allow me to behave destructively either.

There was silence in the room – but I felt no disapproval. I was just going to say goodnight when I became aware that there was definitely something not right. I stopped mid-sentence and asked them if anyone felt cold, and if there had been any problems reported by any of the groups that met there.

Everyone looked at me in some surprise – I had, after all, emphatically said that I was only involved in mind power, and now they suspected I was talking about a spiritual problem. The leader of the group cleared his throat awkwardly. He folded his arms, looking at the floor.

"Last month we had a meeting here – during a meditation, something grabbed our throats and none of us could breathe for about a minute. It was terrifying, but I thought we had dealt with it."

I asked him if he knew if any of the other groups had messed around with raising energies from other dimensions. A look of dawning horror crossed his face.

"Of course," he said. "One of our members tried to raise energy from the floor and we all felt a little odd afterwards."

I could suddenly clearly see in my mind's eye a very strange fungus that completely covered the floor of the room.

"She succeeded quite well", I said. "Pity she didn't use adequate spiritual protection if she was going to mess about in other dimensions."

I come up against this again and again – in vain I point out that one wouldn't travel to Africa without immunisation, so, given that it is possible, why visit other dimensions without adequate preparation.

With great difficulty, I have to say, and using most of the techniques I had learnt from Dom Robert, we eventually dispatched the entity back to where it had come from, but not before it tried again to suffocate the people in the group.

The evening finished after that, and I was aware of many people looking rather strangely at me. What else will she produce from her sleeve?, I could see them thinking!

Those were the last dregs of being an adolescent psychic, and I then proceeded apace with adulthood.

Chapter 6

THE ADULT PSYCHIC – LEARNING INTO PRACTICE

I HAD EXPECTED THAT ONCE I became a mature psychic, I would have no more self-doubts - dream on! I became painfully aware of the responsibility of being able to see 'inside' people, and thus becoming the unwitting custodian of the film of their lives.

I went again to see my clairvoyant friend, Jan, who had seen me through my earlier growth and development. I was feeling rather desperate, because although I was proceeding apace, I really didn't know what to do with my talents. She is a very gifted lady, used regularly by the police to find missing people, and a great-granddaughter of Gypsy Rose Lee. She is also truly majestic, with great presence, and one of the most astute psychics I know.

As I looked out onto her beautiful garden, I was struck again by how many times I had been down to visit her with my tail between my legs, bemoaning the fact that I had no talent, that I was fooling myself, and multiple other things to wallow in self pity about.

She fixed me with her deep-set eyes, smiled at me and said, "Well done, you've nearly made it." For a moment I panicked – what on earth had I done now? Had I stopped the sun in its tracks, created an earthquake in Scotland or turned all tomatoes blue? I stopped myself before I created such an abyss of disastrous possibilities that I would vanish forever more into its depths. I realised that whilst I had been distracted by my extremely foolish thoughts – after all, who has seen blue tomatoes? – she had continued speaking, and was waiting for a reply. I could not think of anything to say; I had not been listening, after all. Fortunately, she continued.

"You are much nearer psychic maturity now than you were last time I saw you," she said.

I thought of some of my recent exploits and thought that she was probably right. I told her of my first 'proper' talk on psychic development. I had hired a room in Isleworth Town Hall, and my local paper had very kindly written a short article stressing the scientific basis of the talk.

When I read the article I was a little daunted – I had told the reporter that my talk concentrated on practical methods of mind control and that I had a scientific background. He had put two and two together and made a mud pie. I am, in fact, indebted to him: he made me clarify my thoughts and be less muddled in my approach.

The audience, thank goodness, was small – about twenty people: a good sprinkling of my supportive friends among them. As I had feared, the article had caused some confusion and many of the audience had come expecting me to levitate and hang from the ceiling like an overgrown fruit bat, produce genies out of my handbag or perhaps turn my audience into rabbits.

("And did you?", asked Jan. I ignored her!)

I think they were disappointed as I proceeded to tell them firmly that I would not be doing any of these things; instead, I would be explaining the difference between a spiritual and a mental psychic approach. I wrote busily and bossily on my flip chart and in my best lecturing voice talked about the practicalities of accessing and using this poorly understood part of the mind. I then became aware that I was being extremely boring, and hastily abandoned that approach.

I wanted to stress to them the excitement of mind development, so I told them of my recent experience at one of the weekly meetings of a breakfast networking organisation. The meeting was held at the God-forsaken hour of seven at my local pub. The aims of the meeting were to promote your business by giving a five-minute talk about what you did, and also to generate business for all involved. At this particular meeting, I had looked around at all the respectable businessmen seated in front of me – the solicitor (beautifully made up and dressed in a tailored blouse and skirt), the accountant (immaculate in his pinstripe and tie), the surveyor (ready for anything with his briefcase bulging) and at my particular friend, the local builder and decorator. What a mixed bunch – and yet, I had to explain what I did, somehow.

When I had first joined the organisation, it was as a digital archivist – a smart name for a consultant on preserving paper records, computer media and photographs. Now I was changing hats. When my turn came, I read out the review published in my local paper. As already mentioned, this had focused on the scientific approach to psychicness. The final sentence had read, "it's a question of knowing what to do. This lecture aims to show people how they can do it – it's all scientific and can be proven to order: you too can learn how to move the earth!"

As I finished reading this, the entire bottle display behind the bar collapsed to the floor with a rending crash. I can honestly say that I shall never forget the look on everyone's face when this happened. They were horrified. There was a pregnant pause, broken by my builder friend hissing under his breath, "Mhairi, behave yourself!" I had started to laugh; I couldn't help it, and within seconds the entire room full of people joined me, albeit rather nervously. I didn't take credit for what had happened - replacing all those broken bottles would have been rather expensive.

After I told this story, I looked around the audience more intently. There were my friends from my earlier 'normal' days, there just to support me, trying to look interested in what I was telling them, but actually planning their evening meals and the best route home. I could clearly see their thoughts, rushing about like little busy bees, and they would have been horrified if they knew in what detail.

Underneath all this, however, what loving kindness! They were, of course, used to my accident-prone life, and did not see anything out of the ordinary in my story.

The rest of the audience, the uninitiated, were looking at me with a great deal more interest, and rather critically. One of the ladies raised her hand and asked if she could pose a question.

"Of course," I said, with some trepidation.

"What on earth use is what you do? Are you forwarding the cause of mankind by being so destructive?"

There were many nods in agreement, and I realised then that I had to pull something out of the bag, or the entire audience would walk out in disgust.

I told them that it was in fact now rare for me to be involved in such mayhem and destruction – I was rather proud of myself that instead of being Madame Nemesis to everyone and anything, I had now taken hold of the power that sizzled round me and caused these mishaps. I thought I should distract them, and spoke about how they could deal compassionately with relationships and improve them and how they could improve their health – all by using their minds more effectively. Ha, I had them now!

I decided, rather defensively, to show them that disasters followed other people as well as me. I told them of my erstwhile experience at the Science Reference Library, when I had been doing some research on bacteria and viruses for an experiment in psychic healing I was carrying out. I had studied pages and pages of pictures, looking for harmless - or even beneficial - organisms that could live in the human body.

I sat at one of the tables, virtuously not being accident-prone. The Reading Room is a vast echoing vault of a room with highly polished wooden floors. If you drop your pencil it sounds like a Chinese firecracker. As I sat there, I became aware of a young man searching the shelves in front of me. Finally, craning his head back, he identified the book he had been looking for. It was on the top shelf, about twelve feet up.

I was helpless to stop the scenario that I knew was going to develop. He looked round for a stool or ladder, couldn't find one, but noticed there was an enormous metal trolley, more suited to carry coal from a coal mine than large quantities of fat books waiting to be filed.

With the agility of a mountain goat, he leapt on to the edge of the trolley and then aimed for the book, intending to use his hand to hook it off the shelf as he gracefully landed on the floor again. He did indeed catch the book, but as his weight came off the trolley, it fell sideways to land with a crash that would make the Last Trump seem like the clash of a child's cymbals. As he descended to the floor, and lay in a tangled heap like a drunken spider, the entire contents of the top shelf rained down on his head.

As he lay on the floor, more unconscious than conscious, the librarian left her desk and tippety-tapped over to him in her high heels. Leaning over him, she brought her finger to her lips and said, "Shhhhhh!" It sounded as if a nest of angry cobras had suddenly appeared in the room and that was the final straw that broke this particular camel's back. I watched with ever increasing amusement as the large collection of readers returned to the various skins from which they had jumped, and replaced their false teeth, wigs and glasses – and huge sobs of laughter racked my body. The librarian, looking more like a mad axe woman than a guardian angel of knowledge, told me to leave and never to return.

As I had by this time gathered all the information I needed, I left with dignity, somewhat spoilt by the laughter that bubbled up and made me snort like a happy hippopotamus. Outside, I collected the poor damaged man, who had interesting bumps all over his head, and we went for a cup of coffee. As I had suspected, he lived a life of accidents and disasters. I explained to him that the problem was too much bio-electrical energy – and suggested ways of harnessing this. If you have the same problem, you will find a solution in chapter 7.

I told him that I had quickly learnt that the path to psychicdom is tortuous and twisting and very strange: progress is extremely slow and laborious for some time, but then suddenly your feet are flying so fast that there is a very real danger of falling flat on your face.

There was a dazed but happy look on the young man's face as he turned several shades of black and blue - it was like having coffee with a drunken panda. I heard from him several weeks later, and his delight was evident... he had cracked it, he said (not literally, I hoped).

By the time I had finished this story, the audience had had enough and left, staggering out like wounded badgers. I had thoroughly shaken their ideas about being psychic and they were not happy about it!

I told Jan that I supposed that this talk had been my first attempt at laying out my psychic wares: an attempt to define my role in life, both at present and in the future. I realised, as I spoke to her, that it is very possible to be an academic psychic, never putting yourself on the line, and fooling yourself into believing that 'thinking' is enough. There is of course no real challenge in this, and it is only by working with others that we can fine-tune our abilities.

When I left Jan, three and half hours later, I realised that I had to get more experience – that I should 'put it out there'! I felt like an exhausted wallflower, but full of determination. For an agreeable change, I didn't bounce down her stairs like an elephant on a motorbike.

Progress – Learning to Live with 'It'

So, I had finally reached psychic adulthood – but there were tremendous gaps in my thinking and learning. Jan had helped me immensely by giving me a vision of success, but the patterns of rejection from my childhood still haunted me. If I was going to be famous(!), then I should be a little more secure, so that when I was slagged off I wouldn't retire into my shell like a shy walnut.

I visited a very good counsellor who lives in Muswell Hill and asked for her help in coping. Now, as I look back at this, I think that I wanted to be patted on the back and told how wonderful I am. The counsellor is a kind and loving lady who specialises in helping emerging psychics, although she believes she has no ability of her own. I sat in her beautiful but uncluttered room and poured my heart out to her. I told her that she would find it hard to believe that I could, and had, fused a set of traffic lights in Roehampton and at all the junction boxes down the street. She looked at me gravely, then observed how inconvenient it must have been for the people trying to get to work. I blushed guiltily – as usual, I had been so wrapped up in my own cleverness that I had failed to appreciate the larger picture.

She is a very gentle but powerful woman, with an innocence that brings forth confidences that might otherwise remain unsaid. When I asked her how she could believe my claims (incidentally, and strangely enough, I do not usually have my word doubted), she remarked that I had turned her lights on and off continually since arriving. I looked at her in astonishment - I hadn't realised

I had done that.

I am very grateful to this lady: she made me face up to who and how I am. One of the searching questions she asked me was how I viewed myself. She told me to imagine looking at myself in the mirror. What did I see? I told her I saw a monster - rather like a bull, with big horns and curly hair. She told me I must change this picture and see myself as a beautiful woman. I'm afraid I snorted derisively. Eventually, we arrived at a compromise: I would see myself as the monster, but with beautiful flowers in my hair – I could be a kind and gentle 'fiend'. But she helped me to be pleased with myself for my development – I had done well, even though my sense of humour still continued to trip me up.

All my life I have been told that psychicness is to be taken seriously – we must appreciate our responsibility to our fellow men: Father Shaw and Dom Robert had drilled this into me, as had the Holy Man in Amsterdam. They had all called me butterfly brain because my sense of the ridiculous welled up at inappropriate moments. Please do not take life too seriously – there are enough disasters and misfortunes to be met without adding to them: being psychic is fun, and if you hear some pompous old (or young) personage who tells you otherwise, don't listen - they are probably only talking to promote their self-image.

Once my interest in the psyche had been roused, I was unstoppable – I read a lot of books, met lots of people, attended complementary health shows in abundance: the quest for knowledge was on, and I wanted to be sure I was A1 Fit and ready for fame when it came. I went for all the Well-Woman tests: it was at this stage that I realised why I had always had such problems with x-rays and blood tests: they just weren't accurate. Every time I broke something, unless I was unconscious or comatose, the x-rays had shown nothing amiss. After my visit to the clinic, I went to a medical herbalist to receive treatment for asthma – a recurring problem. I had my chest x-ray tucked smugly under my arm, and blood test results, all showing that I was in the peak of good health – a veritable paragon of fit womanhood. The herbalist, an attractive open-face lady in her early thirties, looked at me very sceptically, taking in the bulges and sags.

"Rubbish," she said without preamble. Well, I didn't think I was that awful, but there we are. "You've fixed the results," she continued accusingly. "No one in the known universe is average on every test: if I drew a line down the column you would be smack bang in the middle of it."

Well, that put me in my place, didn't it? With a business-like bustle, she pounced on my arm and withdrew gallons of my precious blood (sorry, slight exaggeration).

"Think of something else", she ordered me fiercely. I thought about sad shrews in a thunderstorm. Half-an-hour later, we got the preliminary results. She pounced on them like an angry tom cat. "I knew it," she said dramatically, "you are a walking disaster area – everything is slightly out of kilter... your glands are..."

I held up my hands in surrender, begging her not to go on, I really didn't want to know the details.

She did, however, feel I would survive long enough to make a few pennies as a psychic soothsayer. (Pity I can't do that really, isn't it?)

The Psychic Shows

One of the first shows I went to was held in the Royal Horticultural Halls, Victoria. I attended this with my naughty friend from the Herbal course. She is such a blessing to my ego; she believes I can change the world. I had once demonstrated my legendary skill with parking meters; a meter will appear magically at the point of need, and then it can be temporarily stopped so that time doesn't run out.

Just prior to going to the show, I had failed all the tests for psychic ability during a day workshop in psychic development run by one of our leading colleges. Oh dear, disaster! I was feeling very unsure – somehow, the things I was good at weren't taken into account.

I wonder how many of you reading this book have also attended courses on recognising and developing your psychic powers and have found that you failed to join the ranks of 'psychic workers'. I could not, and cannot, say what a picture is of when handed a card in a sealed envelope. The test is not logical: you don't ask someone to ride a motorbike to prove they can knit! And before anyone says it is a telepathic test, it is not, because the tutor is also unfamiliar with the contents of the envelopes. I cannot say how many teeth the owner of a brooch had left when they died (sorry, that is being rather silly) and I cannot tell what colour is being held to my fevered brow by my working partner (although I can use colours in other contexts). I have come to the sad conclusion that many of these 'tests' relate less to the subject and more to the teacher's ego!

I'm a glutton for punishment, and although I felt like a disgruntled wart hog and was still smarting from my failure, we decided whilst we were at the show to visit the stand of another psychic organisation and have another assessment of psychic ability. Again, I lucked out. I failed every test I was set. The really nice young man carrying out the assessment patted my hand and told me I was a lovely person anyway, I didn't need to be psychic. My friend was trying very hard not to laugh. She is a startlingly attractive lady, slim, blonde and very pretty. Men can't wait to lay down their cloaks for her. I would like to hate her for this, but I can't.

As we left the stand, I turned back for a moment.

"If I'm not psychic," I said crossly, "how do I know that your daughter does not like learning the violin, that you should stop pushing her, that you will not be moving house this year although you think you are – and that you have a black Labrador?"

He went pale, said I was a fraud and accused me of going through his files when he wasn't looking. I have to admit I looked at him with some contempt.

"I am psychic then, in a big way," I said sarcastically, "if I can translocate myself to your office and back – and in the twinkling of an eye." I stalked off in a huff.

We were wandering slowly down one of the aisles when I told Pam that I had to go to the top left end of the hall. I started to make my way down, when there was a loud and cringeworthy hail.

"Aha," said a blond, bearded giant who materialised next to me. "I haf bin waitings for you for some long time. I knewed when you arrived at the exhibition."

Putting a friendly arm round my shoulder, he shepherded me down to his stall in the top left end of the hall.

He took my hand, looked me very seriously in the eyes and said, "You are the most powerful psychic I have ever met."

Perhaps I shall grow blasé one day, but it was balm to my wounded ego and I preened a little. Then I noticed what he was selling. He was selling 'sevenstars', a metal replica of an ancient power symbol. We carried out a whole lot of tests. I could instantly tell him where each star was, wherever he put it, and what metal it was made of - whether tin, silver or copper. I could also describe the symbols on each point without looking at them. I cannot explain at this point how I knew. The power called to me, but it was again a physical power rather than a spiritual one. I badly wanted to buy a sevenstar, but he refused, as he said one of their functions was to be a signal booster to 'mind power', an aid which I didn't need.

This idea of a signal booster has been mentioned many times by the Sceptic. I think it's like needing a huge aerial to pick up a proper signal. Presumably, if I used one I would burn the house down, or at least demolish it, like I did the unfortunate crystals. I'm not sure of the dividing line between signal boosters and 'props': perhaps there isn't one. In chapter 7 I cover examples of props, like pendulums.

So, after attending several more health fairs (slightly less eventful, although they reinforced to me how many charlatans and big 'eads there are in related fields), I decided to become an exhibitor myself. My previous trips into psychicdom had not prepared me for my visit as an exhibitor to a large show held in an enormous and cavernous hall. I should arguably have been ready for the plethora of sights, sounds and colours, but I wasn't. Parking anywhere in the vicinity had been a nightmare, and as I staggered into the hall with trestles for the tables and a large potted plant clasped under my arm, I looked enviously at the beautifully laid out stands of ointments, lotions, oils and strange machinery. I arrived at my bare cubicle pleased that I had listened to my artistic friends and had hired spotlights and bought material to hang on the walls.

TAROT RE

HEDGEHOG POTIONS

Setting up took a long time – far longer than the pre-exhibition two hours allowed to exhibitors. I was so fascinated by my neighbours that I caught myself standing with my mouth open and my eyes bulging. The people opposite me were obviously pretty normal, I reassured myself. As normal as me, anyway.

They offered a new form of reflexology based on colour, and the practitioners smiled at me as they put the finishing touches to their display. Having completed this, they shut up shop ready to go home. 'Shutting up' involved locking a non-existent door and testing to make sure it was locked, polishing the non-existent windows and drawing the curtains. All this was accompanied by large sweeping movements that made me feel slightly sea sick. Having done this, energetic brushing, either of invisible leaves (it was autumn after all) or feathers, followed; the covering of the table at the front was lifted for a moment, then, with a furtive look round, the 'bits' were swept under. I have to confess that after they had gone I had a quick look under the cloth to see what I could see.

I was nearly run over by a large lady in flowing scarves who majestically danced and swayed gracefully down the aisle whilst chanting silently. Her hands ceaselessly scythed through the air as she passed me without noticing my astonishment. There was another stall nearly opposite me that offered a form of Reiki healing. They also looked pretty normal to me, and I tentatively crossed over to talk to the earnest young man in charge of setting up. "What's she doing?" I hissed quietly.

He had been laying out a display of almost fluorescent essences for various complaints, and I noticed he had beautiful hands - built for healing I thought. With a heart stopping smile - he really was rather beautiful, with unruly blond hair and deep blue eyes - he explained to me that I had been privileged to watch a Mexican rain dance. On her second circuit, I tentatively stopped her.

"Excuse me," I said as I stepped out in front of her. "It might be better if you did a Mexican sun dance. If it rains it will affect the number of people coming to the show."

I was totally ignored and she continued on her rounds. The young man glanced across to me.

"You shouldn't disturb her", he remarked mildly. I retired, rebuked. On her third circuit, the rain dance lady stopped briefly in front of me. "Have a bit of reverence", she snapped, in a reassuringly strong Geordie accent.

Whilst I had been watching all that was going on outside my stand, I had not been getting on with the setting up, and I suddenly realised that I had thirty minutes in which to complete what I wanted to do and leave. Hastily I climbed onto a chair and began to fix my beautiful material to the walls. This was accompanied by much swearing, albeit under my psychic breath. The beautiful young man, with a long suffering sigh, came across to help. Eventually the walls were lined with beautiful swathes of material to which I would attach the display of captions and pictures I had prepared.

When I finally left, I was pleased with the results. As I am totally inartistic, my design was rather haphazard, but it worked. I left the show area, noting how many other stall holders were pushing their psychic droppings under the table.

I returned the following morning, my publicity clasped smugly to my chest, and I found that even though I had used enough stuff to stick together the Amazonian rain forest, it had not been strong enough to keep my cloth on the walls. My entire display was lying in a tangled heap on the floor. Fortunately I had allowed oodles of time to sit and examine my navel and calm myself prior to the punters arriving. I felt that my first attempt into professional psychicness had failed miserably.

The young man came to my rescue, again with a huge sigh. He leapt athletically onto the chairs, with drawing pins which he ferociously stuck into the walls. One particularly tough pin was hammered in vigorously using the heel of his shoe. As the entire structure of the row of stands rocked backwards and forwards, I wondered if I should run for it before the whole lot collapsed. Just as he finished and left, a face appeared around the corner.

"I have a rather delicate display on the wall behind you, or rather, I had", she amended sadly. "Have you finished what you need to do?"

I apologised profusely and assured her I had. I didn't dare to tell her that I had still to stick the pictures back on the walls.

For the next twenty minutes I tried every means known to man to stick my display back on the material. I tried double sided sellotape, no go. Ordinary sellotape, no go. Glue, blue tack - forget it. I was in complete despair when the young man reappeared and, before I could stop him, was again hammering drawing pins vigorously into the walls. I have to admit, to my shame, that, as I heard the display in the cubicle behind me fall with a crash to the floor, I fled down the aisle mentioning the call of nature that had suddenly struck me.

I have no idea of what my unfortunate neighbour said to the gorgeous young man, but he was rather white round the gills for quite some time. My display was complete, although my pictures fell off the walls at regular intervals throughout the exhibition. I sat down to await the arrival of my victims. The first day passed in a welter of people as I sat in the front of my cubicle and passed leaflets to the interested and to the definitely not interested. I had never before really taken in how vast is the number of shapes and sizes the human race comes in.

I sat, totally bemused by the large gathering of healers, psychics, complementary and alternative practitioners. I had a stand in one of the side aisles, and that gave me a bird's eye view of much of the exhibition. The colourful and fascinating stands round me kept me riveted for the entire period of the exhibition. Near me was a spiritual healing stand, and there was a continuous flow of the most extraordinary people I have ever seen. I watched, open-mouthed.

One incident I shall remember until my dying day, and possibly beyond. I had been closely and nosily watching the healer as she dealt with her patients. She had started this particular treatment by making dazed bluebottle circles rhythmically in the air: mid-stream, she stopped, her eyes bulged, and a look of horror crossed her face. I held my breath – what on earth was going to happen next? Leaning forward, the healer very gently plucked something from the patient's shoulder. She then examined whatever it was she was holding, and with a look of great distaste, started cracking it between her nails. She then threw it on the floor and smashed it with her shoe. I was absolutely enthralled – had her respectable-looking patient got fleas, or crabs, or lice? Well, she was obviously no better than she should be, thought I, triumphantly. The poor patient was shaking in her woolly socks – she had taken her shoes off – and looked despairingly at the healer.

"Psychic Ticks," said the healer succinctly.

Well, that was the end. I vanished hastily to the back of my stand – a matter of five feet away – and hid under my table whilst I tried desperately to control the hysterical laughter that was bubbling inside me. I did, eventually, manage to control myself and sat back on my chair looking sober and respectable again. Unfortunately, the healer never spoke to me again, because I made the mistake of telling this story to a good friend of mine who had come to see me. With her was her very sad friend who had suffered from the blackest of depressions for the last four years, and was almost suicidal. She hadn't laughed since the onset of her illness, but when I told her the story, she looked at me in amazement and said, in a voice loud enough to frighten wildebeest in South Africa, "Psychic Ticks?" She then proceeded to laugh long and hard, holding her stomach. She left soon after, still laughing, and I could hear her progress down each of the aisles, out of the building and then up the outside; the words 'psychic ticks' came floating back at regular intervals. I can't really blame the healer for being cross with me.

It was at this first exhibition, incidentally, that I became aware of the damage caused by psychic or energy 'vampires': I was feeling particularly tired when I went down to the Ladies. A sweet-faced elderly lady took my arm. "I've been following your footprints down the stairs – you are leaking energy like a sieve." I smiled politely at her, resolving to be careful to avoid her stand, and scuttled into the loo. When I came out, another elderly lady was waiting for me. She repeated the same message, and as she didn't know the first lady, I had to believe her.

I returned to my stand, frowning deeply. What on earth could I do? I thought long and hard, to no avail – I really didn't know what to do about all this. Finally, I sauntered over to the book stall, looked at numerous books on related subjects, but could find nothing that seemed to fit the bill. I tried all the spiritual protections – the blue light fizzing gently round me like an indigestion remedy, the bubble of light that gave me terrible palpitations – and finally staggered like a drunken stag back to my stall, to try and deal with the large amount of people misguidedly waiting to see me.

My clients had a variety of problems, and after they left, I returned to the book stall, more or less satisfied with my wisdom and 'patter', and looked for a book on how to 'centre' myself. I visualised myself imploding, exploding, simmering, shimmering and generally being very egocentric. I couldn't do it. I was so disgusted with myself that I broke another poor inoffensive crystal sitting on the next stall just to comfort myself, and then felt very guilty; it was like eating a very fattening chocolate èclair to make myself feel loved. It was this lack of help that gave me the incentive to develop my workshops on mind protection techniques. This also led me to the Holy Man in Amsterdam, and my inglorious retreat home, with my psychic tail between my legs.

I became a regular stand holder at many complementary health shows, and bored everyone silly with my talks on psychic development. Once I saw my fellow psychics on a regular basis, my tolerance for frauds and charlatans dropped to zero, and I had the greatest difficulty in not intervening and sending the 'offenders' retribution for all the people being taken for a ride. I would love to have turned their hair into seaweed, their cars into pumpkins and to have given them four punctures in their water beds.

As the Sceptic says, many people do seem to need a superior

human being to look up to. One of my obsessions has been not being viewed as a Physical Manifestation of God, with all the ego traps that go with that statement. Actually, I think that this is unlikely, given that I am a rather large tatty lady, but you never know. I was given a very clear example of this need when I was at one of the bigger complementary health fairs. The stands were arranged round the edge of the room and also down the middle. I was furious that my stand on one of the sides was next to a very dodgy organisation adept at using mind control methods. I stormed to the organisers' offices, and then stalked back, muttering darkly to myself: they had refused to move the other stand.

Checking that there was no one around, I stood in front of the stand (temporarily unattended) and, raising my arms, gathered energy and then hurled it in large splashy bursts. I commanded silently that the stand be removed and that the owner leave. I must stress that this wasn't necessary; I was showing off. I could just as easily have sat at my own stall and sent the same power across, but I felt so frustrated that I needed to do it this way.

Two hours later, the exhibitor left the show, and two hours five minutes later, four other exhibitors came up to me, bowed deeply with clasped hands and asked if they could come and learn at my saintly and guru-like feet. They were such nice, normal looking people – shiny hair, attractive clothes - and proper shoes, unlike my rather tatty size $11\frac{1}{2}$ sandals. Again, my sense of humour got the better of me, and I told them they didn't need me, the power was there for the asking, but that they could practise sweeping hand gestures whilst saying "ooncle pooncle broomsticks unlimited". One of the ladies, a serene and very bright 80-something old, looked at me sharply, then questioned me dryly about the function of the words and how they tied into the actions. By this time, I was squirming – drat bright ladies like that! I told her a little guiltily that the words were completely unnecessary, but I thought they might enjoy chanting them. All four left in disgust, presumably to look for another great teacher.

I have found that there is a desperate wish for someone greater to take responsibility for our actions – after all, I had been looking for that myself, when I first started down my psychic pathway. It would have been so much easier not to have to work things out for myself. I have recently realised that the role of master-teacher is fine, but the role of 'godhead' is not – trainees of these God-figures are asked to suspend all disbelief and give up thinking for themselves. I am happy in the role of master-teacher, as I am there to share knowledge in which I am quite accomplished. I am also, however, still very much interested in learning from my pupils and showing them that if they don't think for themselves they will never efficiently develop their mind's psychic powers.

Psychic/Clairvoyant – I think not

From complementary health exhibitions I moved on to psychic fairs. I met many respected and accurate soothsayers during the three years I had been developing, and decided, in 1998, to join an incredibly honest promoter as a travelling psychic consultant and healer. Awfully grand title for what I do, but very enjoyable. We travelled – and still do – in a frolicking way around the country to different venues, me in my psychic garments: a mysterious scarf and long flowing dress. I do not pretend to be a clairvoyant, although I can see alternative futures for those consulting me.

The psychic fairs take place in pubs, hotels, village halls – almost anywhere (well, except the public loos), and all the mystics/soothsayers/clairvoyants/etc. set up round the edges of the rooms and wait expectantly for the punters. This experience has been a great leveller for me – frankly, I am the last choice for any punter. They sit down in front of me and say in resigned tones that as I am the only one available I will have to do. How could my head swell with conceit – now or indeed then.

It is interesting how clients vary from venue to venue: I am usually successful at complementary health fairs, where people are ready and willing to work hard for their health and well-being. At Psychic fairs, they expect the future to magically appear in front of them, complete with all their wishes and desires.

I continue to do these mainly because of the people I work with. All of the other 'readers' are amazingly talented, and two of my particular friends and I have spent amazingly raucous journeys singing either obscene songs or '60's hits at the top of our voices. We have several times been stopped by the police, as they cannot believe that such a discordant noise could come from a group of sober people. Sometimes we continue to sing, and they join in with us, which is novel!!

The psychic fairs are hardly the money-spinners of the month, and whilst I was still waiting for psychic plums to fall into my lap, I decided to fill in the time – and incidentally my purse – by taking over a market stall in North End Road, Fulham. This really was a saving grace to me, and it tided me over until I started to have   clients referred to me.

The Market Stall

We took over the market stall lock, stock and barrel, and sold dried fruit, nuts, beans and herbs and spices. At first we used one of the original barrows, beautifully painted and extremely heavy to pull. After a couple of years, we got rid of the barrow and got a frame stand. This involves setting up a network of interlocking metal rods to which a covering sheet is fixed. Setting up the stall in the morning and dismantling it in the evening was always interesting – my neighbouring stall holders remarked on how often some naughty little imp of wind affecting only my stall would whisk my covering sheet with great speed down the road, hotly pursued by me. A sight not to be missed – an angry rhinoceros in full flight, or whatever it is they do!

Fulham is a multi-racial, multi-cultural area, colourful and fun, and I met some incredibly courageous people, surviving with little hope for the future, and often with severe illness in the home. It was on being faced with this that I further experimented with self-healing techniques, which have proved to be amazingly successful. Mankind is very clever at healing, as well as at destruction.

I met people who dedicated their lives to other people's needs, and learnt one of the greatest lessons of my life from a monk who used to buy his herbs from me. I had set up that morning, feeling depressed at the news of disasters and agony being reported on the TV. I was unable to return his greeting with my usual smile. He took my hand in his and told me gently that I must remember that for every evil deed, there is an army of people dedicated to putting the evil right. It is easy to forget this truth.

Once I had set up, I would sit like the Queen of the May, lady of all I survey. The most surprising and unexpected things happened continuously: one of the most surprising was when an objectionable old man, who was consistently rude when I served him, gave me a brief smile and hurried past. He then returned, gave me a hug and said that he hoped I did well that day on my stall. To say I was surprised is probably an understatement. I was gaping after him like a landed goldfish when one of my favourite ladies took my hand and told me that I had the rare ability to make people behave better than they usually do. What a lovely thing to say, and indeed, in my three years on the market I never had any problems with dangerous customers. I tell this story not to blow my own trumpet, but to encourage all of us who are stepping out briskly on the psychic path. If you can view people's inner workings with compassion, then, in a funny sort of way, they will have nothing to live up to. The down side is that it might free them to behave badly as well

To return to the stall: I was fine-tuning skills I already had both ordinary mental and psychic - when I had one of my sharpest lessons ever. I was talking to a customer, when I became aware that a little boy of about two and half had run away from his father and was heading up the side of the stall towards the busy

road. There was no way I could reach him before he ran out.
Quickly I threw up an invisible barrier in front of him. He hit it
at speed, bounced backwards, and sat down on his bottom hard,
holding his bleeding nose.

Behind the stalls there is a parade of shops. Shoppers walk
down on the pavement between the stalls and the shops. The
people working in the shop behind my stall had watched the
incident and instantly knew I had intervened to save the boy.
They looked at me in horror, and for the rest of the time I had the
stall they only spoke to me to say good morning, looking the
other way. Once again, I have no idea how I erected the barrier,
but when an emergency arises, I can do it. The trick is to see the
emergency coming and deal with it before it becomes an issue. I
would now make sure I tripped the boy up before he reached
the road.

I suppose, in fact, I had already alerted the people in the shop
to the fact that I was a little 'strange'. Before I realised they were
watching me keenly from the back of the shop, I used to screw
up my used paper bags and toss them, without looking, into a
nearby box waiting on the road, between the stalls, for the
dustman. For fun I would bounce them off the next door stall,
or the blind of the shop or just from a great height. They always
went in! Frightened people are not rational, and I had already
sensitised them by my foolishness prior to the incident with the
boy.

Aftermath

I decided to give up my stall just after Christmas 2000, as I was
by then sure I wanted to fine tune my talents more – or perhaps
I should just say tune them! In a way, I had come full circle (I've
always wanted to say that, it's such a cool thing to say), and I
realised that I now had sufficient knowledge to help people take
control of their own psyche and move forward into the future in
a positive way. They would not be dependent on me, but would
gain good health and happiness by self-control and self-

discipline, which differentiates me from other so-called Gurus, to whom disciples need to hang on all the time.

I was also extremely pleased with how well my patients were doing, especially the children. I was beginning to see miracles.

I have shared with you my psychic journey to date – the humour and perhaps pathos of my struggle to deal with the power I have inherited from my mum and dad. Where I stand now, I am supremely happy – I no longer damage, maim and cripple myself or others and the path is beginning to run smoothly. My children are all happily married, my husband gives me loving support and I still have some undamaged friends left.

The next chapter gives details and examples of the use of 'psychic power', followed by some practical exercises that will help you to take control of your own power and access your psyche effectively.

Chapter 7

Down to Business

So What is a Psychic?

As it has been the intention of this book to reach the emerging psychic at all ages, I have covered my life from childhood, adolescence and adulthood (both psychic and physical), and some of the events that can clearly be identified as 'psychic happenings', in the hope that the reader will identify with them, and see the pattern in their own lives. In my own case, I was, despite extensive research, unable to get much help to develop, so I realised that if I was serious about progressing down my psychic path, I'd have to find my own answers. Having found some very exciting ones, I decided to try and formalise the many things I had learnt, so that I could pass them on to others.

One of the things I became aware of very soon after I started trit-trotting down life's byways and psyways (sorry!) was that my trail of disasters did not, in fact, come from a propensity for accidents, but rather from a surfeit of unused bio-electricity. This was confirmed to me in several ways: first, my accidents stopped overnight once I became aware of the problem and used my energy more constructively. (I must confess – darn it – that I have the Holy Man in Amsterdam to thank for making me label and itemise my powers.) Secondly, after some control had been taken, I was no longer stopped by people in supermarkets and told how powerful I was – people could no longer see the electrical 'arc' round me. (Oh dear, how I miss that!). So, once I was no longer a walking nuclear power station, I could concentrate on what I *was* instead. The next task was to try and work out how on earth the system worked, and if possible, break down what I could do into steps. I am, as yet, still unable to do that for everything.

I think I felt compelled to develop my abilities because, having become aware of the life of the mind, I was so vulnerable to the energies flying round and within people… it is like being on the receiving end of numerous simultaneous broadcasts from several different stations, and being unable to turn them off. I think most people have the same problem - one of certain pivotal points that need to be recognised before further progress can be made.

My psychic journey is of course not finished yet – I am daily becoming more of a wonder to behold. (Well, I try.) You will find that, as you progress, you are suddenly able to do the most amazing and wonderful things that you would once have considered impossible; one of the problems is admitting this. I have now started running a workshop, called, rather aptly I think, 'Surfing the Psychic Web', the purpose of which is to help participants open their psychic tool boxes and recognise their abilities.

There is one more point I want to make before we move onto the more detailed stuff. I cannot stress enough that in order to get the brain to act more efficiently on instructions, it is vital to distinguish between *seeing* and *visualising*. *Seeing* involves retrieving the pictures we have filed in our brains. It is retrieving an image that is indexed and labelled, rather than imagined. *Visualising* is when a picture has to be built up and detailed. This technique is used in relaxation techniques and daydreaming, for example, about a nice holiday or a lovely golden beach.

After all the light-heartedness of the previous chapters, this is now the biz, and I am going to be a little bit heavy; just for a page or two! (Or three or four or…) You've reached the nitty-gritty bit.

The first section of this chapter defines the elements that I believe make up your psychic side, and then compares them to spiritual categories. One of my firmest convictions is, as you will have realised by now, that it is important to make this distinction between spiritual psychicness and your own innate mental psychic ability (whether or not you have good access to it).

The second section of this chapter makes a tie-up with the conventional categories of being psychic – telepathy, telekinesis, etc. – where they have relevance to this book. This is not a textbook on psychosity, so I'm only going to cover the bare bones. There are some excellent (and some not so excellent) books that go into great and learned depths of what levitation, holographic projection and 'trans-migrational analysis', etc., are. (I promise you, I really saw that term used, and I don't think it was talking about swallows flying backwards and forwards to South Africa – however, I understood only about one word in three, so it might. I have a wonderful picture of one's soul going off on holiday with its spiritual suitcase under one arm and returning suntanned and relaxed.)

The third section talks about 'energy enhancers' and props.

The fourth section is extremely practical, and gives you exercises to help you develop psychically. I teach these techniques both at workshops and privately. Arguably the most important part of the book, and probably why you bought it in the first place! So let's get on with it and cut the waffle.

Section 1: THE ELEMENTS OF THE SYSTEM

Listed below are the various elements that make up the bio-energy and the spiritual energy systems.

Bio-energy
The human body generates a large amount of electricity whilst about its everyday business of communicating within itself – we are all aware of the sophisticated nervous system that enables us to collect and act upon information received through the five

senses. We are, however, less familiar with our abilities of transmitting and receiving information from external sources.

Unfortunately, we have to a large extent forgotten how to listen effectively to these messages: there has been a breakdown in communication. It is interesting (or I think it is anyway) that many well-known phrases in our language reflect that we are warned by our subconscious when it perceives danger. We are all familiar with at least some of the phrases:

- I smelt a rat
- my skin crept
- I heard warning bells
- that rang a bell
- it left a nasty taste in the mouth

These insights are usually recollected afterwards when events confirm that we should have taken notice earlier. On the whole, we no longer have the instant ability to listen and act on this warning.

It is, however, possible to provide or re-establish an interface between the instinctive/intuitive part of us and the 'higher intelligence'/our conscious mind, so that we can not only listen better to our intuition and our sixth sense but also carry out system and health checks. These checks can ensure that faults and problems within are detected early and that we are then in a better position to carry out maintenance and repairs; taking more control also allows us to enhance the way we manage our bio-energy.

Spiritual energy

Oh dear, I wish I didn't have to do this bit. It is very hard to define and has defeated greater minds than mine! My definitions within this book are:

- God – the Supermind

- Other dimensional powers – spirits, ghosts, aliens and things that go bump in the night (I regularly fall out of bed – but perhaps that would better be called things that "shake the house to its foundations in the night". Sorry, I digress again!)
- Our own inner being – the bit (soul) that inhabits the body and 'ascends' when we die.

The Equipment

Mental psychic ability

1) The brain

- **A transmitting/receiving station** of 'neuro waves' is located within the head. I have heard all sorts of wacky ideas about this – I'm not going to enter into that arena. Suffice it say we pick up unspoken information – and also transmit it. I don't really care if we think it's our third eye (I hope it isn't, eye tests will cost even more), our pineal gland or whatever, just as long as it works.
- **Reference Picture Library**: the filing area of pictures of objects, people, etc. with an index – rather like an illustrated encyclopaedia. I think it is very likely that memories associated with smell, sound and the other senses are subsets of a pictorial record. This library is located in our subconscious. I'm not going to go any further into this – because I don't know the answers.
- **Current Photographic Gallery:** this is part of our consciousness. Large pictures of current events are held here, as are traumatic happenings from the past. The brain continuously processes information and makes judgments and decisions, and pictures scurry through our minds like demented crocodiles. Pictures from damaging situations and experiences especially, are recorded and played back more or less continuously, often interfering with the effectiveness of our memory. Contents from both library and gallery will occasionally fight for attention in our brain.

2) Energy Fields around the body. These are a by-product of the nervous system – like the electric cables in our houses have an electric field round them, so do our nerves. Not to be confused with the chakras (see next section), these bio-electric fields surround and encapsulate the body in seven discreet coloured envelopes. These follow the contours of the body. The colours mirror the colours of the rainbow: they start on the outside with Violet and progress inwards to Red, which is adjacent to the body

3) The palms of the hands are sensitive to energy fields and are physical receptors, which pick up and exchange information, both from people and animals. They can also pick up information from objects

4) The 'Control Room': we all have an 'inner sanctum', or operations centre, within our brain. It is in this room that, in an emergency, we can override automatic/autonomic responses. Deliberate withdrawal into this area is most important in the management of stress, as the body can then get on with its business without our interference. People in a coma, or with other brain damage, also withdraw into this room.

Spiritual Psychic ability

1) The Aura

The aura, in contrast to the electrical energy fields that surround us, looks similar to candy floss when photographed. It is multi-coloured, and probably reflects our spiritual journey and learning.

2) The Chakras

There are seven energy centres within the body – a blaze of many colours. The word chakra is taken from the Sanskrit 'wheel'. Further information on this can be found in many books.

Section 2: USES AND ABUSES

Once again, I must stress that I'm not going to give a dictionary definition of all the wonderful terms that have come into being to describe psy ability. What I am going to do is bring in my experiences to give examples of some of these terms. I shall to some extent ignore my random interaction with my environment – the enormous amount of bio-electricity surrounding me caused many of the disasters that occurred during my life, and should not really be graced with a term other than 'clumsy clot'! But the use of this power to receive, interpret and transmit information is another matter. It is also sometimes quite hard to fit an example into a given category, and there is usually some overlap.

Telepathy

Telepathy has been defined in many ways: I am using it in this book to refer to the ability to receive and transmit thoughts without speaking – and primarily in a pictorial way. There is evidence, I think, that my father had excellent access to this ability from an early age and that, even better, he was able to develop it and put it to very practical applications. A good example is when he transmitted pictures and co-ordinates to my mother. Incidentally, these were not verbal - he just concentrated on transmitting nearby landmarks to identify location. This raises an interesting point – it would have been useless to transmit the information if he didn't have someone to receive it.

My mother also had excellent access to her telepathic ability – it is interesting that she could provide information that my father had not deliberately transmitted: you might say that the dog peeing on the planes incident does not further the cause of mankind, but you never know! My mum was rather more reactive to the pictures she saw than my father was. I have unfortunately inherited her problem of being as impetuous as an angry jellyfish, instead of taking a balanced view.

My father was far less impetuous and perhaps not as multi-talented psychically as my mum was. He tried to find a compassionate solution to the problem of German planes dropping their bombs on our airfields. You may recall that he set up a 'virtual reality' airfield for enemy aircraft to bomb. He must have had a very clear picture in his mind of an airfield he was familiar with, set up a false location for this, and then transmitted this information to enemy planes flying overhead. He also managed to set up a 'data audit trail', showing pictorially the destruction caused by the bombs. I think it is even more gob-smacking that he could also train other people to do the same things. I wish incidentally I had learnt to do this – I could get pigeons to drop their eggs on my neighbour's cat when he is trying to catch my goldfish.

I shall return later to the concept of 'intervention': my mother was very reactive – she would mete out justice to 'offenders' at once if she picked up that someone was being naughty. You will recall that she 'knocked' the misbehaving jockey off his horse. My father, on the other hand, taught me to be passive without being weak – to try and take the heat out of conflict and be an observer rather than become one of the players involved.

I will be mentioning later some of the children with learning difficulties that have been referred to me: these difficulties might be magnified by the uncontrolled reception of people's emotions, and the hypocrisy we are all guilty of. "Lovely to see you Penelope", we say, whilst thinking, "Damn, I haven't done the washing, I wish she hadn't come." This kind of thing is a big contributory factor to the turmoil some of these children suffer – especially those with access to telepathic ability.

Remote viewing

When I started to research this ability, it was like opening a cupboard door to take out a shirt and the entire contents of the cupboard falling on my head, completely burying me! Oh dear, oh dear! If you search under 'Remote Viewing' on the Internet, you too can be deluged and overpowered by the wealth of information available. Disappointingly (you might say), I'm not going to tell you how to watch aliens at their breakfasts or how to pluck incidents from the past and 'transmogrify' them. (That's what I mean by opening the cupboard door!)

For ease of reference, and because I think it is a rational division, I have split my explanation into two parts: the first part is closely related to telepathy – and overlaps, I'm afraid. I am treading carefully round a minefield here – where does telepathy end and remote viewing of people's inner thoughts and memories begin? Telepathy involves the deliberate emanation of thoughts; Remote viewing, in this context, is a conscious decision to 'walk in and have a look'. This can be done on three levels: a) scanning of the information held in the energy fields surrounding the body; b) accessing and viewing the *current photographic gallery* – the conscious mind; c) accessing and retrieving information filed in the *photographic library* – the subconscious. The second part involves the viewing and collection of information in a wider context.

Part 1: People Power

a) Scanning the energy fields

Although I have already mentioned the energy fields or envelopes that surround us, I have not yet spoken in much depth about those that steal energy from these fields (psychic vampires) and how bad it is for them to do so. This is because the fields are polluted by our hopes and fears, and also because they carry a record of illness whether diagnosed or not, so that the vampires will pick all of this up together with the energy. In the last section I will give you exercises that show a method of scanning or remote viewing someone else's energy fields. When a patient is referred to me, one of the first things I will do is to check out the information held there.

b) Accessing the Current Photographic Gallery

As I have already said, we have a large collection of detailed pictures of recent and traumatic events and happenings from the past, held in our conscious memory, usually by negative emotion. I have mentioned that whilst I was attending my first course on intuition I became conscious of a Jewish man's thoughts. I could see how sick his son was, and also see clear and detailed pictures of where he lived. Obviously, such information was very present, so that the pictures were very clear. This information was not deliberately transmitted.

c) Viewing the Reference Picture Library

As I have already explained, this is the filing area of pictures of objects, people and places, with an index – rather like an illustrated encyclopaedia. Viewing this part of the subconscious is always intrusive and can be felt by the patient. You may remember how upset the Sceptic was when I wandered about in her mind and accessed these images and memories – she said she felt like the rummage stall at a jumble sale.

To clarify the issue, let me give you an example taken from the earlier chapters. When I intervened in a knife fight that was about to take place in a car park, I could clearly see the anger and hurt in both men's energy fields. After I had registered that, I could also see, in both men's conscious memory, details of the robbery they had been involved in and the subsequent harrowing experiences they had faced. Finally, accessing their filing system in the subconscious, I could see details of their family backgrounds – the fact that one of them had three children, and that the mother of the other lit candles for her son.

My mum, as you will no doubt have realised, was an expert at accessing other people's memory banks. She could clearly see many details about the jockey she knocked off the horse – that he was unkind to his wife was her justification for intervening, but I'm sure she could see many other things going on in his life as well!

Part 2: Collection of information from other sources

This second part involves the viewing and collection of information in a wider context. I am again on shaky ground here, but I believe that when I access 'secret' locations to retrieve information, I am not picking up this information from anybody's mind but, like a camera, I'm just taking pictures with my mind. It is interesting that when I have intruded into some fairly dodgy locations (yes, I value my skin and I shan't say more!), then warning sirens have gone off in that area: my energy is somehow detected.

Remote viewing, as developed by intelligence agencies and government organisations, often uses astral travel or projection of the spirit to gain information. As I understand it, this 'astral projection' involves sending the 'spiritual body' out on a mission whilst the physical body remains behind. The two are joined by a silver cord, and if this gets cut or damaged by a psychic scissor man, then bad luck – the traveller becomes a cabbage. Information is collected by the observer from whatever site he or she has visited and, upon return to the body, it is relayed to the controller.

Telekinesis/Psychokinesis

This ability involves using the power of the mind to move or change objects, to give a dictionary definition. Throughout the book I have talked about both deliberate and very undeliberate telekinesis: it is probably the most easily accessed of all the psychic powers. My attention was drawn to this skill when I met Father Shaw and he raised and lowered a mug using his mind. When the Sceptic and I were experimenting with matchsticks in a bowl of water, we had not realised that, as I had not taken control of my psychic energy, I was myself a walking telekinetic firework (if there is such a thing!). The disasters that tripped gaily through my life were due to my uncontrolled interaction with pretty well everything around me.

My mother was an expert at this skill – sorry to mention the poor jockey again, but it was telekinetic energy that brought about his downfall. Thinking about it, she was a fine one to criticise me for interacting so violently with my immediate environment! At least, I usually only brought about my own downfall rather than everyone else's. Unfortunately, I got the punctures, rather than any bad guys round me!

I think telekinesis is really one of the hardest areas to be specific about, it is so wide ranging. One of the most famous experts in telekinesis is Uri Geller who speaks about rearranging the molecules in a spoon. I think this is achieved by some kind of emission from the brain (like a laser), and, if this is so, then psychic surgery – you will remember the case of Lucas's damaged blood supply to his legs – uses the same beam. It seems to me that there are two different ways in which telekinesis works – the first way, a permanent way, by changing the structure of an object. The object then remains changed until the molecules are re-arranged again. The second aspect of telekinesis does not cause permanent change, and works by interacting with the surrounding energy field of an object.

When I was a little girl, I'm fairly sure that I did indeed use telekinesis to unlock doors, so that I could escape from nursery school. This was a temporary effect – the locks were undamaged and could continue to be used. The second example of this is when I opened the car door in my local supermarket car park in an impossible way – neatly bypassing the wing mirrors on both our car and the one next door. Again, there was no damage to either car, and it was just a temporary effect. I have a confession to make here; I probably did dislodge the hornets' nest in my first foster home, and direct the hornets down the chimney, but that might be merely wishful thinking!

There are many more examples in the book of what could arguably be called telekinesis, but I'm only going to include a couple more. I have mentioned that I can change part of an x-ray so that it doesn't show any problems. In every other respect it will look like a normal x-ray – it's rather clever that I don't just blank it. I'm obviously much smarter than I realise, because I can also change the results of blood tests so that all readings are normal for whatever test is being carried out. I'm actually not sure how this works: whether I change the composition of my blood whilst the blood is being taken, or if I change the sample afterwards, or in fact if I interfere with the machine making the analysis. When I was having a consultation with the medical herbalist, she asked me to think about something else and we then got a true reading. As an aside, I think many of my interactions with my environment were caused by 'subconscious telekinesis'; if there is such a thing! My energy fields and possibly rather random 'emissions' brought accidents raining down on my head (sometimes literally).

Psychometry

This is the reading of emotions and facts from an object. Everything we come across has its own electric field, which is also a recording surface. By tuning into that energy field, we can read the object's history.

On the whole, paper is not a good recording surface, but metals are. My clairvoyant friend, Jan, is regularly used by the police to try and find lost children – by tuning into the energy field on an item of clothing from the child she is able to give information to the police. She is usually able to tune in on the child's energy field and say where he or she is. Another example of this ability is when I picked up the illnesses of previous clients who had lain on the crystal healer's couch. It was also possible to pick up information recorded on the packets of the herbs that were passed around during one of the weekends of my herbal diploma course.

Intuition/Sixth Sense/Gut feeling

I have already mentioned this in passing at the start of the chapter. There are two elements to it – first is the ability that our subconscious has to pick up information about damaging situations and people that are bad news to us. The second element is the ability to listen to this information. This is usually what we fail to do; and this is why we so often find ourselves saying, "I should have seen it coming," after the fact.

It unfortunately became apparent during my first course on intuition that I am about as intuitive as an umbrella. My husband, sickeningly, is excellent at it. He is also very smug. It is a joke in my family that if I urge a certain road to be avoided because of a traffic jam ahead, then whoever is driving will make a point of selecting that very road – there *never* is a jam. Never mind: I'm quite good at cutting my toenails.

Farseeing: the telling of an event in the future before it happens

I have to admit that I have not yet sorted out how the future works. Incidentally I do believe it is possible to cross time: it is likely that déjà vu is a skip forward then a return to the present. I have spoken to many of my clients about glimpses of the future, and how to interpret them.

I think that, on the whole, the future is far more flexible than we realise. When I intervened in the knife fight, I could clearly see two futures – one, that the older man would die and so would the younger one later, and in the second case, that neither would (well, not immediately anyway). I could also clearly see two futures for Diana's mother – if she had not gone away with her boyfriend to Mandalay, she would not have been killed in the car accident. Presumably, if she had also not hired the Austin car, or had travelled elsewhere, the accident would also not have happened.

You will remember when I told my friend Suzie that her sister was pregnant, and then, several weeks later, broke the news to her that Caroline had lost the baby. (This was not telepathy as Suzie did not know this.) One of the big headaches of far seeing is not being able to differentiate between past, present and future.

It is no good warning someone that they will break their leg, when in fact they did it a year ago. I live in hope, on the other hand, that the future that the GP and the gypsy saw for me will come to pass, think of how many people I can help if I become better known.

Psychic Surgery

The general term 'Psychic Surgery' is used to cover a multiplicity of things. When I looked it up on the Internet, I realised I really must make my meaning of this term crystal clear. I believe there are three different aspects to this: One, the psychic surgeon route, where a spirit rider inhabits a medium's body for long periods at a time, so that surgery can be carried out using the knowledge the spirit rider had gained in previous lives. The spirit is usually that of a dead doctor or surgeon. The therapist often has no recollection of the time spent in surgery. I think the operation is carried out on the ethereal or virtual body and that this is mirrored in the patient's physical body. It sounds very spooky to me!

Secondly, there is the surgery carried out, psychically, by a 'witch doctor'. They apparently have the ability to modify the molecules in their hands to match the molecules of the patients, thus permitting entry, and a good rootle in their patients' bodies.

The third aspect is the mental approach. One of the reasons why I was conducting my research at the Science Reference Library was that I had been 'remote viewing' the contents of a biological warhead. Having carefully taken a mind picture of the bacteria, viruses and other nasties involved, I then checked through literally thousands of enlarged pictures, until I found an organism that was as close a match as possible, but that was fairly harmless. Having identified this, I then 'changed' the contents of the warhead. I have also, to a very limited extent, used my mind to operate on illnesses where arguably I cannot do any more harm. In the case histories in the next section, I will talk more about the use of psychic surgery in changing cells 'in vivo'.

Other 'ilities' and 'athics' that don't quite fit in the mould

It is quite sensible, on the face of it, to try and squeeze my experiences into known categories, but when I consider various incidents that happened, that is not very satisfactory. Sending headaches to someone (the vicar when I was nine), or ill-wishing them (my friends who did not come to my party) are wild cards which don't really fit any of the categories given above.

I'm also not sure what category the meter changing/sticking episodes fall into. Useful, probably!

I would also like to mention my interference in other people's energy fields and transmissions. When I have been asked for help because someone is being drained and damaged, I have often, in my mind, placed the bad guys in a plastic crystal – to all intents and purposes, this shuts them down, and their energy fields, instead of being round the body, are suppressed inside. This is a potentially very damaging thing to do.

I think the silver cap placed inside my head by Father Shaw had a similar function, but because it only covered my head, the rest of my body was free to continue bouncing about like an excited gooseberry. There are other aspects of being psychic that do not neatly fit into any given category, but are often mentioned in passing – enlightenment should hopefully be given in the case studies. This concludes the second section of this chapter – I hope you have found it edifying!

Section 3: ENERGY ENHANCERS

I am not going to mention – or even attempt to mention – all the energy enhancers and props used to 'boost the signals'. I am reasonably familiar with the following:

Crystals

Crystal healing workshops are held, at which body, mind and spirit are worked upon. It is believed by some that all stones rocks and gems are inhabited by a sprite or angel. If this is the case, I have made an awful lot of them homeless when I smashed their houses with my mind. I think it is more likely that the crystals enhance, record and transmit information. You are probably aware that crystals were used to enhance signal strength in the original wireless sets. You will recall that I became very sick after being treated by a crystal healer; the guardian crystals had faithfully recorded the ailments and problems of previous clients. Clear quartz is a particularly good amplifier. People who sell crystals will tell customers to buy the one, or ones, that they are drawn to. This would imply that crystals vibrate on different frequencies, and harmonise differently with different people. I have many clients who have been given crystals after attending a workshop. That crystal, already vibrating on their frequency, was further attuned to their energy fields. Sadly, this energy flow might only go one way – some workshop organisers use the crystals to download energy from participants back to themselves, the little sweeties. I will talk later about a particular client who became very sick after attending such a course. I do not believe it is enough to cleanse a crystal with salt water after it has been attuned to somebody.

I have had a very chequered career with quartz crystals. Actually, I lie; handling them has been a one way ticket to destruction for them and, as I love to hold them, this is a problem. So far I haven't been very successful at modifying my power as I look at them. Lately, apart from having a little colour drained from them, other crystals and gemstones have survived

Dowsing

I have started to use pendulums and divining rods in my workshops, as they are, again, energy enhancers. Participants seek the answers to questions, and the pendulum signifies 'yes' or 'no' by swinging in a certain way. I believe in fact that the diviner already has the answer, but the pendulum gives him the confidence to access this knowledge. It is, again, a method of linking the instinctive/

intuitive part of us to the higher cognitive brain.

Tarot Cards

I believe that tarot cards, too, enable access to the information known by the inner self. I am able to influence the cards in a spread and ensure the ones I want come out, so it is unlikely that there is a spiritual entity involved. In fact, once when I was with my friend Jan, the same cards kept coming up, until I realised they didn't mean what I thought they meant. As soon as I stopped interfering, completely different cards appeared in the spread.

If I want to really annoy a clairvoyant friend of mine, I say Tarot cards are just props. Actually, I don't think they are, I think they are powerful enablers.

Sand Readings

Now, this really was an eye opener. I had been keeping a hawk eye on one of my next door psychics at one of the fairs, when I noticed she had a plate of sand in front of her. She invited me to place my hand in the sand and then press down. When I lifted my hand, there were some nice deep indentations that would have made an ant dream he was Lawrence of Arabia. Apparently the sand picked up information from my energy field: and it was surprisingly accurate. She was a pretty fey lady anyway, and, once again, I think the sand enhanced what she knew already.

I am not going to mention all the other paraphernalia of psychicdom – if you wish to read a cockerel's innards, or forebodings in fishes' scales, fair enough. But I shan't tell you how!

Section 4: THE TECHNIQUES

In order to realise our full psychic potential, we must learn to manage the resources within us first.

PROTECTION

Introduction

I have mentioned in the previous section that bio-electric fields surround the body. These are generated by the nervous system. These fields consist of seven discreet envelopes closely following the contours of the body, and mirroring the colours of the rainbow. The outside envelope is Violet, followed by Indigo, Blue, Green, Yellow, Orange and Red, which is next to the body. These fields are very susceptible to energy loss and theft from psychic vampires. We often start to lose energy faster than we can generate it – the symptoms of energy starvation are, at first, cold hands and feet and tiredness. The second stage is a fluttery, apprehensive tummy, and the third is palpitations and faintness. Fortunately, although these envelopes can be damaged, they can also be repaired. I am going to suggest some exercises that will help to make you more aware of your fields, give you techniques to protect them and show you how to donate energy.

FEELING THE ENERGY

Exercise 1

This exercise should be carried out with someone else present.

Select a wall in your home or at work that is uncluttered. If there is furniture against it, move this. Make sure you're not going to break your neck over a carpet or rug. You should carry out this exercise with the light behind you, so that you are not still picking up visual clues. Stand between three and four metres away from the wall and shut your eyes. Walk steadily towards the wall until you feel you can walk no further – you will have encountered the energy field of the wall. This might feel hot, cold, like a barrier, but you should be able to feel something. (Mind you, if someone tells me that, I automatically can feel nothing – I just hope you aren't as contrary as I am.) Please make sure the person with you stands by the wall, to give you the confidence to know you aren't going to brain yourself.

Exercise 2

After a few minutes, repeat the previous exercise, but walking backwards towards the wall. The energy field of the wall usually feels quite different. Do ensure that your partner in crime is standing by the wall again.

Exercise 3

Now that you have experienced the energy of an inanimate object (please repeat the exercises until you do), we will progress to feeling the energy of a fellow human being. I would suggest that you get someone to supervise this exercise as well. Stand about 3 metres away from your partner in crime. With your eyes shut, walk slowly and steadily towards each other. When you feel the presence of the other person, stop. The point at which you'll feel this energy field can vary: closer or farther away from the body. Once you have stopped, open your eyes and, with your hands, push gently against this energy field – what does it feel like? The third person in the room is only there to prevent a head-on collision!

SUPPRESSING ENERGY FIELDS

Exercise 4

I would like you to see a greenhouse in your mind's eye – preferably without plants at first. Please note, you must *see* this, not *visualise* it. If you are unfamiliar with one, and can only vaguely remember what they look like, this technique won't work. You can familiarise yourself with a greenhouse either

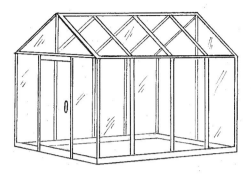

through a gardening programme or by visiting a large garden centre and looking at display models. Why a greenhouse, you may ask? In Western culture, the greenhouse is associated with growth and protection – cold winds are excluded, the frost cannot harm the plants and predators are kept out. Needless to say, the greenhouse must be functional and not a beat-up wreck with every pane smashed! This exercise is divided into two parts.

a) For the first seven days

In the morning, when you get up, in your mind walk into the greenhouse and shut the door. You can have a chair in there, or whatever will make you most comfortable. You should then stay in there until the evening, when you come out, either on your return from work or when you go to bed. This will keep you from losing energy. After seven days you should feel a bit more energised and you won't need to spend all day in the greenhouse anymore.

You will, however, probably feel isolated during this exercise – you are no longer picking up subconscious signals from others – but please persevere for the week. You may also find that the prime energy stealers in your life are wondering what's happened to their between-meal snacks – the energy canteen has shut down. Many people will be quite unpleasant when this happens, in an effort to make you release some more energy for them. I'm sure we have all experienced the extremely personal remarks people make for no apparent reason.

My mum, before I mastered this technique, drained me until I could hardly walk, let alone think. She would look at my tummy and remark that fat people were very unlovely, weren't they? Immediate emotional response, more energy released. After a few minutes, she would say, "Nobody loves fat people, you know." Again, immediate response, and more energy going her way. The final remark, after about half an hour, was "You'll lose Norman (my husband), you know – he'll find someone less ugly." That was the killer, and I would leave and go home like a very sad lamprey. (I'm not sure what that is, but it sounds sad, doesn't it?) I must stress and stress again that she did not realise what she was doing and didn't actually mean what she was saying. She had no recollection afterwards, although she obviously was worried about my girth on some level. The vast majority of people who steal our energy don't mean to do it; it isn't intentional, so that there should be no judgment against them. The idea is just to stop it happening because it's so bad for both parties.

b) Forever more!

You are now on a maintenance scheme. You will probably have become aware of the people that usually drain you because with raised energy levels comes increased perception. When you spend time with those people, go into the greenhouse before contact if possible; if not, as soon as you can. When you meet new people, make a note if you begin to feel drained, and immediately go into the greenhouse. After the first seven days, you can come in and out whenever necessary…but please don't forget to do it, or you will return to your first drained state. It is, of course, far better if our energy can be protected rather than restored.

There is nothing mystical about this – the brain will take your use of the greenhouse as an instruction to shut down the energy fields, or suppress them, so that they are inside the skin, rather than on the outside. Once they have been suppressed, no one can steal your energy.

You may well find that, if you persevere and use this technique as an effective tool, your greenhouse begins to fill up with plants without your conscious volition. This is because your brain is rather happy to have a place of safety. If you forget to come out of the greenhouse, you will stay there – no harm done, but you may well wake up at 3 am feeling very hot and sweaty. Just come out and shut the door.

One of the wonderful 'side-effects' of this protection technique is that when we suppress our energy fields, we are not so easily perceived. We do not become invisible, of course. If you are travelling late at night, or are somewhere that you feel vulnerable, go into the greenhouse and you will be safer. You may recall that when I was a very young child, I hid in a wood from a rather dangerous man. I used the expression "I became one with the bush" – what I did in fact was to instinctively shut down my energy fields, so that he wouldn't notice me, and he didn't! This was not a conscious decision, and the deliberate techniques given here are far more useful.

Protecting your family

Unfortunately, bullying at school (and in the work place) is on the increase. The adult members of your family will be able to use the greenhouse effectively but I suggest a slightly different technique for children. I would also like to suggest an effective preventative to help children resist the many childhood ailments that rampage through schools.

Exercise 5: Child Bullying

Many children, at some point, have problems with bullying by other children at school. This is usually about energy stealing. I am talking about the gut-wrenching fear of going to school knowing that you will be ridiculed, or threatened, or actually physically abused. This technique has proved most effective for the children who have come to see me with this problem.

Before your children go to school, tell them to clearly see Darth Vader costumes. They must carefully put the costume on, and be able to hear themselves breathing like Darth Vader does (children must be familiar with 'Star Wars' – borrow the videos if necessary). In case you are worried that your children might be picking up a negative role model with this, bear in mind that they usually know that in the end of the saga, Darth Vader becomes one of the good guys. If they don't, tell them!

When the children return from school, they should carefully take off the costume and put it on a chair, ready for the next day. This must be repeated until it is obvious that the bullying is decreasing.

Exercise 6: Child Medical preventative

Many children that come to see me have autoimmune problems. They are frighteningly vulnerable to every infection going round at school, and often spend a long time at home, ill. Children who are normally healthy can also hit a cycle of recurrent illness, and should use this technique to break the cycle. Before the child goes to school, clearly see a surgeon's mask in your mind's eye. There are many medical programmes with operations being carried out where these are used. Make a careful note of how the mask is tied on, and then *in your mind* carefully place it over the child's face. Most children are happy to do this themselves, but it is important that you give them backup, by also seeing the mask on them.

One of my patients is a child with cystic fibrosis who hasn't had a cold or flu for a year. Her mother and I are convinced this is because of the mask – through its use, her brain has been alerted to the fact that damaging organisms will be coming her way. The previous winter, she had spent long hours on the nebuliser and suffered almost continuously with a very dangerous pneumonia bug.

Exercise 7: Protecting your house

As you will be aware after doing the first exercise with the wall, your home is surrounded by energy fields. It is important to learn how to shut these energy fields down: people who have used this technique for a long time have commented that even if their home is in a high-risk burglary area, they have not been broken into, although their neighbours may have. Again, it is not that your home becomes invisible; it just isn't noticed.

You should be able to see a bivalve sea mollusc clearly – an oyster at a pinch, but a giant clam (with the ridged shell) is better. Put your home – whether house, flat, maisonette, etc – inside this shell. The hinged bit is at the back of the house, the open side at your front door. The sides should bisect any wall you share with neighbours, and if you are in a flat, the shell should pass over the top and under the bottom – this technique only relates to your space. The outside of the shell can be rough and wrinkly looking, but the inside is mother of pearl – you can see lovely colours in it. The shell will remain in place until you remove it.

When you go to bed, or return to your home and everyone is in, you can shut the shell by seeing the top meeting the bottom. If you do this whilst someone is out, they may well have problems fitting their key in the lock.

Exercise 8: Protection from spiritual/psychic attack

After you have come out of your greenhouse, you are of course vulnerable again to psychic attack. Just before you go to sleep, it is helpful to again shut down your energy fields. This has the added bonus of giving you protection from spiritual vampires. In films such as 'Casablanca', there are the most amazing mosquito nets – huge affairs, often three meters high. If you can see these, they are the best, but if not, then see the smaller kind from other films, or which you may have experienced on holiday. The mosquito net must completely cover your bed, from floor to ceiling. The drapes must fall gently against the side of the bed, where they are easily accessible to you.

Having established the net over the bed, crawl in under it and close the gap. Just before you go to sleep, knock your elbow, foot or head against the side of the net. You will see a flash of 'lightning' spread from that spot to surrounding areas. This looks like the static you can build up on nylon bits and pieces. This is something you should do to reassure yourself that the spiritual protection is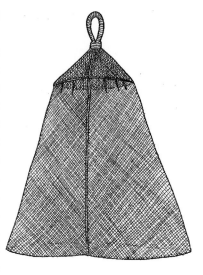

there as well. I'm not sure how this works, but I have had good feedback from people who commented that they are no longer going walkabout in their sleep, and that their dreams have improved greatly.

Exercise 9: Saying goodnight

This may not be a very logical place to put this, but it does tie in with a quiet night's sleep. When you have finished a relationship, or are being pestered by someone who won't accept 'no', just before you go to sleep, see that person standing in front of you. Quite deliberately, look them in the eye and say, "Goodnight, I'm going to bed." Smile and turn around and see the person looking at your back. There is no rejection, with possible guilt trips, going on. You are simply establishing clear boundaries between you.

ENERGY 'DONATION'

So, having stopped all that energy stealing, you are now going to give energy to those who have stolen it – whether you love, hate or amiably dislike them!

I must stress again that most energy stealing is not deliberate. One of my seven year-old patients explained to me why she believes that once you donate energy, the recipient will no longer try to steal energy from you. As Eleanor explained to me, it's like being so thirsty that you will drink from a puddle on the pavement, even if a dog has pee-peed in it. But if someone offers you a drink from a clear stream, you would prefer to have that.

RELATIONSHIPS

Protection is all well and good anyway, but so far we have only talked about defending ourselves, not about improving the situation for the long term. Unless we change the scenarios, our particular energy stealers will always be around when we forget to go into the greenhouse, or after we come out.

Exercise 10: Improving relationships

Either in the morning or evening – make sure you are not in the greenhouse – you should carry out this exercise. As I said earlier, you will have become aware of those people who make you feel drained and tired. See that person standing in front of you in your mind's eye, about three metres away. Now see a candle flame – just the wick and where it enters the candle. Think about something beautiful – something that took you by surprise and moved you deeply. I saw a child of about three sitting outside a shop waiting for her mum. Out of the sky, a white feather drifted gently down. The little girl watched it falling, then held out her hand. The feather landed on it. She sat as still as a statue, hardly daring to breathe, an expression of wonder on her face. Then the wind picked up the feather and it floated away. She laughed, clapping her hands. I have that same feeling of wonder when I see a rainbow or hear certain pieces of music. This feeling is a bonus. Re-experience it; with practice, you will be able to place it with the candle flame, and watch the flame travel down a very thin trail of gunpowder until it reaches whoever you want to give energy to. The purpose of the gunpowder is not to blow the person up; it is just a carrier for the flame!

As the flame arrives at the person, say, "Here you are, this is a present for you." There is no hypocrisy in this technique – you are merely passing on a gift that was given to you. Within a matter of days, you will become aware of an improvement in the relationship. Mind you, this is not a charm or a magical solution for all your rapport problems. Repeat this procedure for each person you want to give energy to. People have asked me why this must always be done away from the person's physical presence, and also why you can't simply see yourself touching the other person. In either case, you would be sharing all the hopes and fears stored in your energy field instead of giving a purer energy that mends.

TRAUMATIC MEMORIES

When we have had bad experiences in the past, we tend to keep large, clear pictures of the scenes – they remain in our current photographic memory, kept there by strong negative emotion. The problem is that they affect later relationships and eventually can totally baulk our memories altogether – we run out of storage space. I found out the other day that when you delete a file on the computer, all that happens is that the heading is removed – the text remains bobbing about on the disk. In most cases, these old snippets are written over by new files or programmes. Sometimes, however, these old files can cause problems, slowing up the processes and eventually causing hard disk crash. I think this situation is mirrored often in people who suffer from senile dementia. I have, in these cases, carried out the following technique for them, as they lack the concentration to do it for themselves.

Exercise 11: Dealing with the past

There will be both recent and far past memories that surface in your mind. Every time they do, freeze the picture as if you were watching a still on a huge cinema screen. Repeat Exercise 10, but this time, see the candle flame travelling down the gunpowder until it reaches the screen. The flame arrives at the screen, touching the bottom part of it. As it arrives, look again at the picture on the screen and say, "Here you are, this is a present for you." The picture will slowly fade, and you should see the screen behind. Do this every time you think of something with sadness and bitterness – what happens is that once the negative emotion is released, the picture will become a small icon, like an image on a microfiche. The memory has not gone, but it is no longer interfering with your thought processes.

I think one of the key things to remember is that unkindness and cruelty are sad, rather than bad. Keeping this in mind helps take the heat out of any situation.

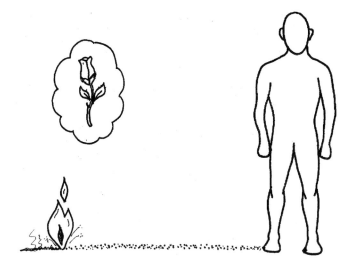

RELATIONSHIP LINES

I am, in fact, only going to touch on these. Really, the only reason I am mentioning them at all is because of the current culture of dealing with them. You don't really need to think about them when giving energy – the previous technique is enough.

Exercise 12: Seeing the lines

Everyone that we have a relationship with – whether good, bad or indifferent – is linked to us by a cord or line. Starting with those to whom you are close, shut your eyes and see them standing in front of you, about three metres away. With practice, you will see the line that connects you. It can be joined at any point on your body, and any point on theirs, although it tends to be the head, chest or tummy area. What do you think the line is made of? How thick is it? What colour is it? Does it feel healthy?

Once you are confident you can see the line, repeat this with the other people in your life. I think you will be quite surprised. This is an information-gathering exercise; you do not have to do anything about it. If you use the candle flame technique in Exercise 10 with each of these people, check occasionally and you will be surprised to see the lines changing in composition, thickness and texture.

I beg of you, do not try and cut these energy lines – this could seriously rebound on you. I always think of the newborn baby – it can die if the cord between it and the afterbirth is severed without tying it off. Cutting the ties that bind you to another can make you seriously ill.

Before I leave this section on relationships, I would also ask you to try and resist the temptation regularly mentioned in complementary therapy books to see your hands covered in mirrors. This is supposed to greatly help by reflecting back bad thoughts and energies. Well, I don't know about you, but I don't fancy a game of psychic table tennis with the ball whizzing back and forth with ever-increasing velocity.

HEALTH

This section covers health issues – techniques are given to help maintain the health you have, improve on small glitches (often to do with stress) and finally help you deal with major health problems. I must stress here that none of the techniques should be seen as alternatives to medical treatment you are already receiving – they are complementary. This is not just a statement put in so that you don't sue me, but because I believe us complementary therapists have got to work more closely with the medical profession.

a) Maintaining your health

I have been struck by the fact that we have fairly elaborate health checks for our computers to remove corrupted data and clean up our hard disk. We also have virus checkers and system failure warnings. We are less careful with our bodies. I think that everyone, once a year at least, should carry out the exercises in this section.

Exercise 13: Colour Wash

As you already know, the body is surrounded by seven coloured envelopes – these mirror the colours of the rainbow and are a by-product of the nervous system. Violet is on the outside, Red on the inside. These energy fields get depleted, often by energy vampires, but also by illness. I would also like to add that I have had stunning results from people with seasonal disorders (lack of sunlight). Instead of doing the exercise once a year, they do it every day during the winter months. When you get up in the morning, and before you go into your greenhouse, stand by your bed. You should clearly see a bucket of paint next to your bed (if you can't clearly see the colours of the rainbow, get a paint chart). On the first day, the colour in the bucket is Violet. On the second day, Indigo, on the third, Blue, on the fourth day Green, on the fifth day Yellow, on the sixth day Orange and on the seventh day Red. Please don't try and be clever and do two colours in one day – the brain knows paint takes a time to dry, and it will mix the colours up together in a random fashion.

Picking up the bucket in your mind, pour it over your head and down your body. Please remember that we are talking about 'seeing' rather than doing – I don't want to have to pay for your new carpet. If you are especially drawn to a colour, this is probably because you are deficient in that in your energy field. Repeat that colour for two days.

Exercise 14: Colour fixing

There is another technique that is helpful to top up your energy fields. You should assemble scarves, swathes of material or wools to cover the colours of the rainbow. Put these on a table and shut your eyes. Shuffle them round and pick up a colour, in any order. If you are quite severely lacking that colour, the material will get hot in your hand. Put this colour to one side. Without opening your eyes, continue until you have held all the colours, one at a time, again putting the ones that get hot on one side. When you have completed this exercise, open your eyes and make a note of the colours that got hot then, when you go to bed, place them under your pillow for a week.

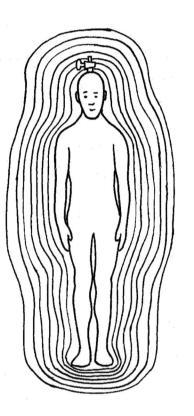

Exercise 15: Cleaning the system out

I'm not sure whether it has always been the case, but nowadays, infectious diseases such as chicken pox, mumps, etc. leave a residue of bacterial and/or viral contamination. These can severely affect our health and make us prone to further infections. Glandular fever, meningitis and hepatitis are also bad news, and urinary tract infections and food poisoning are the total pits!! The brain doesn't seem to be aware there's a problem and the following exercise is designed to raise its awareness.

I would like you to clearly see a transparent rigid plastic figure – this is called 'Anatomical Man', a doll into whom you can insert kidneys, liver, heart, and so on, in their right places. If you can't see this, the drawing on the opposite page will do.

Stand by your bed. There is a tap attached to the top of the figure's head. When you turn it on, the water starts to fill the figure up from the bottom, like with a watering can. The water slowly fills the figure, pouring over into the arms when that level is reached. You will probably notice that the water is gently swishing about when the figure is full.

What you should also notice – again, children have no trouble with this – is that somewhere within the torso of the figure there are black, white or colourless wriggly things. If you try to look hard at these, your rational side will cut in and tell you not to be ridiculous. Lift the front of your foot and watch the water drain out. Repeat every day until the water is clear. Once the brain is aware of this residue, though, it will wash the system out and probably send in the army to clean up the 'saboteurs'

STRESS MANAGEMENT

A tape/CD of relaxation exercises is available from the publisher.

Exercise 16: Tweaking the system – small malfunctions (migraines, neuralgia)

This exercise is an example of a very specific way of dealing with a given problem. It has no relevance to a fungus infection of your right big toe, for example. The brain really has a hard task coping with our pollution-ridden environment and the stresses and strains of modern day life. Because of this, migraines and neuralgia have become more common than ever, and these are linked to allergies and other problems. This exercise will deal with some of the pressure.

In the morning, before you go into the greenhouse, clearly see either a deep-sea diver's helmet, or an astronaut's. Because of news reports, it is common knowledge that one of the problems with using pressurised suits is that the body expands – it takes advantage of not being subject to gravity in the same way. Several of the earlier astronauts came back with fairly severe health problems because of this.

Pick up the helmet in your mind and see yourself putting it on. As soon as it is fitted, you will hear the pressurisation hiss. You will be aware of looking through a glass,and it may feel a little claustrophobic. Try and ignore this, you are only going to wear it for ten minutes or so a day. After the 10 minutes, take the helmet off and put it on the chair, ready for the next day. The brain will become aware that the bones of the head are rather tight and will take the helmet as an instruction to expand these, thus helping with both neuralgia and migraines. Repeat for five days or until feeling better.

c) Major health issues

I must stress again that most of my techniques for seriously ill people are individually tailored to suit the individual and the problem. This exercise is one you can carry out to improve communication between the body and the brain. It has been helpful to people suffering from motor neuron diseases, but can be used in a wider application.

Exercise 17: Re-establishing communication

Again, whilst not in the greenhouse, see a tree you are familiar with in your mind's eye. An apple tree is particularly nice, I think. Once you can clearly picture it, place the trunk of that tree up your spine; the roots will travel down your legs into the soil. The crown of the tree is in your head. When you first use the tree, see the branches and twigs as bare – it's winter, if you like. After a day or so, notice that buds and leaves are beginning to appear. Watch these develop until you have a tree covered in nice green leaves and blossom. Every day, for the next month or so, longer if you have motor neuron disease, see the rain falling on the leaves, followed by nice warm sunshine. The water and by-products of photosynthesis travel down the trunk until they reach the roots. You then should see the water and nutrients from the soil being transported up the trunk to the crown of the tree. You will probably not know the details of 'translocation' in a tree – I've forgotten most of what I know – but the brain will still understand what you are asking it to do – improve communication.

ALLERGY DETECTION

This is a large and complex area, and I'm only going to touch on a technique for listening to your inner voice when it tells you to steer clear of a substance. There are two things to bear in mind:
  1) that at some level you already know what you are allergic/sensitive to; this exercise provides an interface between logic and instinct! 2) I have an extremely allergy-ridden son; he is worse at some times of the month than others. The exercise I'm going to give you will enable you to check over a period to see if the level of allergy changes.

Exercise 18: Finding out the biz

Go to a chemist that stocks essential oils. Pick up a bottle – these are usually brown – and hold it in your hand, with your fingers curled round it. Shut your eyes. The colour you see behind your eyelids will tell you whether you are sensitive to that oil or not. If you see a light colour – pastel colours – then you are able to use that oil. If you see a dark colour, stay clear. If you see a mixture, then your sensitivity will vary through the month. It is very difficult to explain the difference between visualising, seeing, and this colour wash. The only way I can explain it is that it is like when you sunbathe with your eyes shut. The light penetrates your eyelids and you will probably either see the colour yellow or red. When you are checking for allergy, the colour is similarly behind your eyelids. You can find what other substances you are allergic to by using a clean empty essential oil bottle and putting wheat, eggs, etc. in it and again checking the colourwash.

REMOTE VIEWING – TECHNIQUES

Once again, this is a complex subject and I'm only going to give you a taster, just to give you access to your psychic toolbox. The next two exercises tie in quite well with healing, and are very useful, as you can build on them.

Exercise 19: Scanning

For the first part of this exercise, you need a friend or relative that has known health problems. Cancer sufferers should, if possible, not be used, as they are already under enough stress and worry. Stand in front of your subject. You are going to use the palms of your hands to give you messages about health problems. Stand at a distance to permit you comfortably to pass your hands over and around their bodies. You are not going to touch them (unless they're a very good friend, you'll get walloped if you try), but position your hands about five inches away from their body. You will notice, either at once or with practice, that your hands register cold, heat, numbness, and so on, over the part of them that is giving them problems or which is the original cause.

I had a friend that asked for my help as she was about to have her right elbow taken to pieces (not literally, I hope), cleaned and put back again. When I used the scanning method, my hands got very hot over the back of her neck. I told her that she had severely banged the back of her head about 20 years before – it was an old injury. She denied this, and said she would surely remember if something had happened. Nevertheless, I stepped into my role of healer and placed my hands over the area. The next day she rang me, having spoken to her parents. At the age of 14 (21 years before), she had fallen backwards off a child's swing, knocking herself out on a metal bar behind. I visited her again the following week. During scanning, my hands got hot over her shoulders (not, interestingly enough, her back). She confirmed that a few years previously she had had a car accident.

Because subconsciously she was trying to protect her head, she had held her shoulders rigid. Again, I gave her healing. Finally, a couple of weeks later, when I scanned her, my hands got hot over her right elbow. She is right handed, and of course the elbow took a lot of punishment. We had several healing sessions and she finally made a full recovery without the operation. Do listen to your hands – they will faithfully give you information.

If you want to progress in this ability, you can of course repeat this exercise with a wide range of people – both those who are sick, and those who appear to be fit. Have confidence and listen to the message you are hearing. I will not delve into healing here, but there are many healing courses and books that give information about sharing God's gift of healing.

Exercise 20: Scanning related to psychic or mind surgery

This exercise is closely related to the previous one. Carry out the scanning technique given, but this time, when your hands let you know there is a problem, try and identify what it is. This is the starting point I use to carry out psychic surgery. You must familiarise yourself either with one of the Options Menus on your computer, or with the schematic diagrammes used by technicians. In both cases, there is a general index from which to make your preliminary selection. If you are looking at a car handbook, you first identify the likely problem areas: for instance, if it's fuel starvation, you will look up the carburettor, possibly the petrol pump, and so on. Assume you are familiar with your car's innards. You are sure the problem is the carburettor, so you take it to pieces to clean it. If a new part is needed – perhaps a gasket – you can go to the motor factors and buy it.

The procedure for working with people is very similar. Prior to carrying out the exercise, I would like you to either draw or use an Options menu. You should have all the major parts of the body written on horizontal tabs across the top of the page. As with the computer, when you select one of these tabs, a vertical menu appears with the component parts listed against white squares. Check each box and see if there is a tick in the box. You must take your diagnostic tool one step further. When you select one of the ticked boxes, a drawing or plan of that part appears, again with a white square. I'm going to divide this exercise into clear steps. I am also going to create a scenario, for convenience. The patient you are seeing has a heart condition – he has a very irregular heartbeat, which is controlled by a pacemaker.

Step 1: As soon as possible after the consultation begins, carry out a preliminary check. See the preliminary page of the Options Menu in your mind's eye. Are any of the tabs already highlighted / selected? Make a note if they are (in this case HEART and possibly KIDNEYS – the adrenal glands may be involved).

Step 2: Carry out the scanning procedures of the previous exercise. Do not pay special attention to the heart area at first – get a general picture. Again, check in your mind's eye: are any tabs depressed on the menu? If they are, keep a note.

Step 3: The heart area should have been confirmed as a problem. Scan this area again, this time with the drop down menu for HEART. On the drop down menu will be a drawing of the component parts that make up the heart – all the valves, the arteries, the veins, the flippy floppy bits etc. The parts of the heart that are giving the problem may already be ticked – your brain anticipated and ticked them while you weren't looking. If not, check each entry and ask yourself if there is a problem. Listen to the first message, as that is the most accurate. You can even tick each box in your mind and see if that feels right, but I think that's a little excessive!

As we are dealing with a specified problem, you will now know that your patient is in trouble, say, with the vagus nerve misfiring, and this is causing the palpitations.

Step 4: Look at a medical book and clearly identify the vagus nerve. Now, concentrating on the picture, see in your mind's eye a severed high voltage electric cable that is waving about in the ai,r showering sparks. See yourself approaching the cable, dressed in a heavily insulated suit. You take hold of the cable, and carefully re-unite it with the end to which it was originally attached, carefully connecting each wire in each phase. When you have finished, carefully bind it with tape. You should notice that the lights in the room that were flickering before are now shining steadily. This technique will tell the vagus nerve to fire more regularly. I suppose one of the reasons I use this illustration is that I speak from personal experience. My entire family suffers from irregular heartbeats and bumpings, thumpings and flutterings. All the rest of my generation are now on pacemakers. I, having used this technique and perhaps a couple of others, am not, and rarely have any problem – unless I'm deeply upset.

This chapter has necessarily been rather heavy, but I hope you have found it informative and useful.

Chapter 8

CLIENT NOTEBOOK

THIS LAST CHAPTER DISCUSSES some of the people that have come to me with their problems – both health and emotional – and how they used their own innate abilities to take more control of their lives. You could call these case studies, but I hate being called 'a case' (usually a nutcase, I'm afraid), so I shan't bother.

I have, over the several years I have been practising, seen a large number of people. Rather like when knitting a complex pattern, there are certain constants – the material, the needles, the pattern. However, the design can vary enormously. In the previous chapter, I have shared some of the basic methods I use; these are supplemented with additional techniques where necessary.

There is neither the time nor space to mention all my patients here, but the following cases stand out in my mind. The names have been changed, but the details haven't. Finally, I have not gone into deep and meaningful medical details of any of my clients – I have a feeling I might blind you with science if I did!

Client 1

Freddy came to see me when he was 11 and a half. He had an inoperable tumour on his pituitary gland. He came to see me via a friend of mine, who was appalled that he and his father had decided not to have radiotherapy treatment: the consultants had told them there would be a reduction in 'brain power' after treatment, and that he could lose between 20% and 40% of his intelligence. His memory span would be shorter, and he would find learning new things harder, if not impossible. However, the prognosis without treatment was bleak.

I persuaded Freddy and his father to have the treatment, as I was sure that I could put a damage limitation on the side effects of the radiotherapy. As I'm sure you are aware, the pituitary gland is 'the leader of the orchestra'; it co-ordinates hormone production of all the other glands. With no pituitary gland left – it would be destroyed by the radiation – Freddy had also been told that he would never grow beyond his current height. Finally, he would never achieve puberty – the sex hormones would not be developed or released.

Freddy was a paragon of virtue – he did everything I suggested. In May and June 2000, he received radiotherapy, administered over seven weeks. Twenty minutes before he received each dose, Freddy went into his 'control room'. We all have this central sanctuary – I have mentioned it several times before in this book. I had told him to see in his mind's eye a room that he was familiar and happy with. In the room was a comfy chair he sat and read in, and in front of the chair was a roaring log fire. He also had a cup of hot chocolate by his chair. The room he selected was his bedroom but when I said that we had to line it with lead, to warn the brain what was coming, he asked, diffidently, if we could put the lead round the outside of the room, as it would look pretty ugly on the inside. This we did.

Once he had completed the radiotherapy treatment, he started on other mind techniques. I told him he had to be able to faithfully reproduce a torture chamber in his mind: he got a video out on the Spanish Inquisition. He paid no attention to the harrowing story line, but he made a detailed study of the chamber itself. He could vividly reproduce in his mind's eye the rack that stood at the corner of the room, and to which he was tied, spread-eagled. The inquisitors went about their business, dwarfed by a huge inferno. Every now and then, one of these hooded figures would come over to Freddy and ask him if he would confess to some crime or other.

Each time Freddy said, in a loud voice, "No, I cannot." The inquisitor would then tighten the rack up a little bit, stretching Freddy's body. (He said this was actually rather painful, but there you are, we have to suffer in the cause of science!) The final technique I gave him was to by-pass the conventional hormone production route, and get his brain to intervene directly. Freddy said he thought this was rather like hotwiring a car. That's often how thieves steal a car, he explained, by by-passing the ignition. I looked at him a little sharply, he sounded so knowledgeable! I'm not going to give any more details of this last technique, but please contact me if you want to know more.

I had various reports during the year after treatment and then, exactly one year later, Freddy rang me in a state of high excitement.

"Well done, all," he said. "I've just had my final assessment – my intelligence, memory, reasoning ability are all unimpaired." He gave a large sigh of happiness.

"Also," he continued, "I have grown four inches in the last year, and there are beginning to be significant levels of male hormones in my blood." Just before he hung up, he told me that he had just come overall top of his class in recent exams. After I put the phone down, I was filled with a deep feeling of humility that I had been able to play a significant part in his recovery.

Client 2

Tommy came to see me when he was eleven: he was small for his age, pale and skinny. As he was a reasonably severe diabetic, he had to inject himself with insulin every day. As he stood in front of me, I used my mind to check his pancreas, and realised that it was damaged. Tommy had become diabetic straight after having chicken pox. As I have already said, unfortunately, infectious diseases – viral and bacterial – do tend to hang around in the body for a long time, if not forever, and can interfere with many of the body's functions. The solution I found was to get Tommy to by-pass the damaged 'mechanism', and get his mind to directly take charge of insulin production.

I first asked Tommy if he could see, in his mind's eye, a cow's udder. He looked at me, speechless.

"Well, to be honest…" he said.

I cut across what he was about to say. "Go to the library and look at a picture of a cow and memorise it, so that you can faithfully reproduce its udders in your mind at will."

I hurried on, as he opened his mouth to protest. "Also, go to your dad's garage and look at the battery charger for the car."

Tommy was familiar with this, as they had just had big problems with the car's battery. He nodded, and pictured it. I then told him to milk a cow in his mind, to actually feel the udder in his hand, and to see the milk coming out of it. Tommy was looking at me with reluctant respect by now. I explained to him that a regulating mechanism was also needed, otherwise he could have too much insulin – the brain would override the damaged 'automatic' system, and would not have feedback to know how much insulin was needed.

A battery charger, of course, measures how much charge there is on a battery: when the needle remains on the left after the battery is connected, the battery is fully charged, when it swings to the right, it is flat, and needs charging. The battery charger, in Tommy's case, would provide the feedback by measuring how much insulin was in his blood. I told Tommy to check the meter several times a day. If the needle was in the middle of the dial, then he did not need to milk the cow's udder (the system was under reasonable control). If the needle was to the right of the dial, then he must milk the cow's udder, checking to see when he had done enough. If the needle was on the left, however, then he must just leave everything alone until the insulin levels dropped. Children instantly understand that you cannot change the reading on the battery charger directly, it is merely a display, like a computer monitor screen that can only be accessed through the computer. Tommy faithfully carried out the exercises, and he also continued to carry out the conventional tests to measure blood sugar. Eighteen months after I first saw him, he had had no insulin injections for a year at least.

Client 3

One of my first cases, Bobby, was brought to my attention by his distraught parents. Bobby was 21, and had been in a deep coma for several months, after a severe head injury in a car accident. I am not an expert on how hospitals evaluate brain damage but, on the basis of his scans and brain waves, the doctors had decided to turn off his life support machine. When I went to see him, he was lying like a marble effigy, and at first I thought there was little I could do.

One of the problems that people with head injuries have is that quite a lot of their neural circuitry may be damaged, and it is necessary to establish new 'pathways' for the brain to use. Using my mind, I enter the patient's control room. By the door there is a fluorescent blue tennis ball. Opening the door, I pick up the ball. Outside the room is an unused corridor – rather like that of a multi-storey car park. As I throw the ball down the corridor, this changes to that of a beautiful 5-star hotel's - flowers at the end, pictures on the wall, plush carpets, soft lighting and so on. When the ball reaches the end of the first section of corridor, the passageway bends to the right, at an angle of 90°. The ball can only be thrown down one section at a time. After each section is done, I return to the control room, and so does the ball. Once a corridor has been changed, it stays that way, so that it is only necessary to walk to the end of the last completed section and throw the ball again. When I repeat the exercise the next day, the new passageway I will open turns to the left. After this, the right/left pattern is repeated on alternate days, until suddenly one day I find myself in a main lounge or reception area. Enough new circuitry has been established.

The very sad ending to this story is that although Bobby went from strength to strength, one day I had a call from his parents.

They were very grateful for my help, they said, patronisingly, but as they were both pillars of the local church, they did not want any details relating to my work with Bobby revealed, and they would take legal action if I did. What hypocrisy, and worse, they have cut off so many other people from perhaps learning from a fellow sufferer with first-hand experience of these techniques.

Clients 4, 5, 6 and many more!

Leukaemia is on the increase. More and more children are coming to me for help. So far we have a convincing batting record, the kids and I! At the time of finishing this book, the four children I have been seeing the longest are in spontaneous remission, and are fit, healthy and playing football! There are variations on a theme, but the main techniques are as follows. The children are told to see a coral reef, with fishes swimming about them. As they watch, the coral reef grows as on a time elapsed film. Every time they do this, the brain instructs the bone marrow to either grow more, or to convert more to producing red rather than white blood cells. Telling the children to see a lava lamp in their mind's eye further reinforces this. The background oil is clear, but the bubbles are red, and shaped like coins. These red bubbles of course represent the red blood cells, and rise from the bottom of the lamp to the top. This is, again, giving the brain instructions. I am particularly happy to see these techniques working.

Client 8

When I first met Miriam she was 6 years old. Her mother, a beautiful high class Indian lady, had called me in to give healing to her daughter, so that she could emerge from the safe and hidden world in which she lived. As I arrived at her elegant house, I reflected upon how desperate she must be to ask me - outside her culture and her religion - to help. I felt very humble, and determined to do my best for Miriam. When I was introduced to Miriam I immediately became aware that she was a bright intelligent person trapped in a twilight world. Contacting her was like talking to a goldfish ,swimming around in a bowl. Periodically she would swim to the side of the bowl, and peer at me, and even contact me with a smile or a frown. Then she would withdraw. My first meeting with her was inconclusive - I watched as she ran and danced round the room, occasionally stopping to listen to hidden music, or to look at unseen pictures. What a beautiful little girl, I thought again - beautiful hair and skin and a smile with amazing warmth... but, for the moment, only reachable for a few seconds at a time. I left the house feeling extremely baffled. What on earth was going on?

When I visited the family a week later, Miriam's mother was pale and drawn; she had had a very bad week, as Miriam had been violent and very disturbed. The problem had begun when Miriam and her extended family had gone to a hamburger restaurant, to celebrate a child's birthday. Miriam enjoys hamburgers, and was happily humming to herself eating, when suddenly she clapped her hands over her ears, and started to scream silently. Her mother noticed that another family had arrived, and were standing some distance behind Miriam table. As a loud quarrel erupted in this other family, the child's screams became audible. It had occurred to me in the week after I met her, that perhaps Miriam was a powerful telepath and was severely affected by the thoughts and pains of those around her and the scenario that week seemed to confirm this.

Prior to talking about this to her mother, I carried out a couple of tests myself. Miriam was withdrawn, standing in front of me rocking to and fro, her face blank. I knelt in front of her, and pictured a large soft fluorescent green ball. I cupped this in my hands. Miriam looked at my hands and then at my face. Carefully I threw her the ball, and saw it travelling slowly across to her. She clapped her hands, and screamed with laughter. I repeated this several times. By the end of five minutes, she had lost interest, but during that time, her eyes had followed the ball as it came towards her, and she even tried to catch in a couple of times. I was absolutely delighted - but to make sure that telepathic contact was indeed the way we were communicating, I decided to carry out another test. Typical blooming scientist I suppose! I asked her mother to show me Miriam's favourite biscuit. Closely watched by Miriam I held it up and then walked back to my seat. In my mind, I put the biscuit on the shelf behind me, although I was actually still holding it in my hand. Immediately, she climbed on to my knee and checked the shelf. She looked sadly at me when there was no biscuit, and tugged my hand whilst looking at the kitchen cupboard. I then, of course, handed her the biscuit.

I wondered how on earth I was going to explain this to her mother - it sounded so bizarre. As I explained the problem as I saw it, we both also saw the horror of Miriam's situation. Body signals can be at odds to verbal messages and confuse us, but how much worse to know there is a conflict between what is being thought and what is being said: also to know that people either pity or fear you because you are different.

I wish I had succeeded in helping Miriam to emerge from her hidden world: her parents' religion made them believe that her illness was a judgement from God, and shortly after I began to see real improvements, she was sent to India to be raised by her grandparents. I wish I had reached the level of knowledge I have now, because I could probably have helped her more successfully – or at least, on a shorter time scale.

Client 8

It is interesting that there seems to be a batch of patients that come to me with the same problems. Shortly after I met Miriam, another little girl, called Mary, was referred to me. My association with her confirmed to me that telepathy is pictorial – there is a database of pictures with captions to aid retrieval.

Mary is the daughter of successful and well-to-do parents. She lives in a large house in a salubrious part of London. On my first visit, her father, a well-known and respected barrister, opened the door to me. John is tall and fair-haired, with an engaging smile and open countenance: I had to revise my bad opinion of barristers as sharks and piranha fish, as I fell under his charm like a sea urchin succumbs to an octopus. He invited me into his beautifully and warmly furnished living room. His wife, a successful artist and writer, greeted me with a somewhat desperate smile. Mary was sitting on a pile of large cushions in front of a roaring open fire. She is a small elfin girl, ethereal and gentle. Her expression was curiously flat and disinterested, but she got up politely and said good evening. I had been asked to help her, because she was having severe problems relating to her form teacher and was starting to show signs of wanting to withdraw into her own world. I watched her settle back down on the cushion.

Her father, embarrassed by her lack of interest, asked her to go and me a drink. "Sure," she said in a dull monotone. As she passed me to go out of the room, her gaze sharpened and she looked hard at me. I took her hand. For a timeless moment, she stood completely still, then she turned abruptly and left the room.

Her mother, a vivacious, pretty woman looked at me hopefully.... "Can you help her?", she asked me. Whilst Mary was out of the room, her mother explained about the school problems, and that Mary had spent many hours with two child psychologists: I was horrified to hear that they had told Mary she should picture digging a hole and then burying the two teachers that were giving her grief, so that they would be unable to trouble her. Before I could comment, Mary returned silently to the room, handed me the drink with another sharp look, and retired back to the cushions.

After she had sat down, I tried to explain to Mary's parents that her problem was the rest - or most of the rest - of the human race. She did not have a problem herself. We talked for many hours that night about learning to handle being psychic. I gave Mary a series of exercises to help her to cope with the people she came in contact with. We talked, in detail, about her teacher, and I then added another exercise that I believed would help her to deal with the situation. I explained to Mary that it was in fact the teacher's problem, rather than hers, that Mary could read her thoughts.

I asked Mary what things she particularly liked – she mentioned several, including feeding and watching the birds in her garden. She confirmed that she knew her teacher also enjoyed wildlife, as she had said so often in class. I told Mary that when she returned to school, every time the teacher looked at her or asked a question, she was to clearly see her garden with the birds bustling about in it. She was also to hear them singing in the background. I impressed upon her how privileged she was to have the ability to help people by using her gift. I also agreed with her that she was a monster in some ways: she had the power to interfere and destroy people's lives. Her parents blenched as I said this, but I sensed Mary was sick of people pussyfooting around and pretending they thought all was well. I told her she was also an angel, on a mercy mission for mankind.

It was a most informative evening. I had made contact with a fellow psychic, albeit a very young one, and I had learnt how to capture some of the elusive ideas and feelings associated with being psychic. I could even put them on paper. Just before I left, we had a final conversation. Aware that time was running out, we were perhaps careless. We returned to the problem of her teacher, and the problems Mary was having with her. The conversation proceeded:

Myself: "She had problems......."
Mary: "And she has only just found out, I know, but...."
Myself: "You can't, you know that."
Mary: "It's very hard sometimes, isn't it?"

Her mother at this point, burst into tears. "My poor baby,"

she sobbed, "she can't even think coherently any more...".

Mary and I looked at each other, and it only then dawned on us that most of the conversation had been carried out silently, and pictorially, in our heads. (Incidentally, the highlight of her school report three weeks after she returned to the school, was her form teacher's remarks that "Mary had started to communicate lucidly and fluently and was now an asset to the school." I have to say, both Mary and I had a good laugh about that.)

Final part of the medical cases

Before we move on to other things, I'm going to tell you about a lecture I gave to some prominent doctors on using the mind to heal yourself. After waffling learnedly about the identification and treatment of various ailments, I mentioned the bacteria and viruses that can rampage through our bodies: I asked them to accept the premise that it is possible to use the brain to 'photograph' these organisms, and then change them into something else less harmful. That being the case, to what should I change them?

I looked a little complacently round the group of assorted specialists - this should be interesting! A great time of learning for this humble psychic, I felt. There was a murmur as they discussed the matter between themselves, then three people put up their hands, and proceeded to have a ferocious argument about whether visualising the dangerous viruses and bacteria as candy floss was more effective than ice cream or flowers. I was speechless for a moment, my mind literally slipped a cog, and I was left open-mouthed like a large herring on Southend Pier. If you listen to your gut feelings in this, you will probably immediately have thought 'how ridiculous'. I agree - and even more – how illogical. The brain can only make changes if it believes they are possible, and logical. Not only that, but I don't particularly fancy a bunch of flowers in my right kidney.

When I finally got my brain back in gear, I have to admit I

looked at my 'intellectual saviours' and told them very coldly that I had just spent three weeks researching bacteria at the Science Reference Library (after which time, of course, I was banished from the premises for ever). I tried to explain that visualisations are invented and composed by the brain, but that seeing gives clear instructions. Perhaps needless to say, I failed to convince them – even to try the methods out.

Non-medical clients

Client 9

One of my clients was a beautiful Spanish girl; she had come to me in tears because a clairvoyant had told her that she would never marry, and never have children. As she was 43 and didn't have a boyfriend, this seemed entirely possible. I promised her – rashly – that if she would carry out the procedures I gave her, she would marry and have a child. (Please, please before you put this book down in a scandalised fashion, may I reassure you that I would not make such a promise now... no way!!)

The clairvoyant had looked at her future and seen that, as a result of her abused childhood – brutalised and sexually assaulted by her father – she could not allow a man to approach her without screaming inside. I spoke to her of the pictures that we carry in our heads of past trauma and despair: in her case they were huge Technicolor photographs from her past, kept in the forefront of her memory by the emotions of pain and fear. The techniques I used I have already mentioned in the previous chapter (the green house and the candle flame/wonderful feeling). These helped her to change these huge pictures into small icons, thus freeing her from the bondage of the past, and also giving her more space in her memory banks. Every time she remembered an incident, she would freeze the picture, and then send the flame and energy present. Additionally, she always looked her father in the eye in these pictures, and said to him, "How sad you had to behave like that." The net result was that when I saw her two years later she was married, and gloriously pregnant. She told me, with a smile, that after she had dealt with her feelings towards her father, she had carried out the same exercise with her mother, who had been too frightened to intervene. "I never want to see either of them again," she said, "but I'm free of fear now." Phew!

Client 10

Another client I had was via recommendation. I had arranged to meet Dolores in a coffee shop in Portobello Road. This had temporarily become a focal part of my life. It was there that I learnt of aloneness on a grand scale, of broken dreams hidden behind laughing eyes, of the colour of suffering. The café is without a doubt, the anchor sheet on which much of the local community depends. It is run by a God-fearing Syrian who cares deeply about his customers.

Indeed, many of my patients congregate in the café – in atmosphere and colour scheme, it could either be an aviary in London or a Parisian pavement boudoir. I met Dolores outside and sat down at her table and began to take down her case history. As with most of my clients, she was elegantly dressed and well made up. I became aware almost immediately that there was a shadow behind her, and that her dreams were not sweet. The shadow was of death, but not of her own. The data coming in those days was so very raw.

We spoke of her life and her experience. She had just arrived from Dublin, and was now setting up her own clinic as a psychotherapist. We talked of psychic awareness, and of the dangers of being unprotected. I still did not know there was a difference between mental and spiritual protection, but I was aware that yet again this was an important meeting, and I wondered what I would learn from it. After chatting for 15 minutes or so, she mentioned that she had written her life story, a book that had received international acclaim. It was about possession of a house and a ghost. I am to this day not really sure who was the possessor, and who was the possessed; the whole situation was so tightly woven. I would like to be able to say that a thousand bells rang in my head and that there was instant recognition of the title.

After our long chat, at which I was completely out of my depth, we arranged to meet again and I assured her I would think long and hard about the ghosts that haunted her waking hours, and tormented her dreams too. We never did – she returned to Dublin, and shot her husband who had somehow become 'the ghost' in her eyes. If I had the wisdom of today (limited as it is even now), I could have warned her and perhaps helped her to prevent this tragic outcome. Moral: only tackle cases that you know you can help with. I should have referred her to someone else.

Client 11

I once helped a woman called Freda, who had a large black snake haunting her (thereby hangs a tail – forgive the pun). Through Freda I met John, a GP. John asked me if I thought I could help his wife, Gill. She was in hospital again, under restraint, as her schizophrenia was out of control. She had been ill for 12 years – in and out of hospital, and in a straitjacket frequently. This is another warning tale. Just before she first became ill, she had visited an organisation in Glastonbury, and had attended a course on psychic development. I must say, when I looked in her mind (remotely, of course) at what she had experienced, I was gob-smacked... the poor wretches that attend my workshops have a very boring time in comparison.

I didn't at first believe what I was seeing – and in fact hearing - in Gill's mind. This poor scientific psychic was unable to comprehend why it would be necessary part of the course she had attended, to have a sheep in a tutu, a silver cord hanging from a tree branch, or why there was a coconut on a table surrounded by tinsel. The ladies in charge of the workshop were dressed in diving suits and danced energetically past the sheep and the coconut. The hard stamping of the feet made me wince...

how bad for their backs. The 'singing' was something else – it reminded me of a mating tomcat or tortured bagpipes... Still, there was power there.... raw, fundamental power to enslave and ensorcel. Once I could feel the power, I trod very warily indeed.

At some point in the psychic weekend, a control mechanism had been inserted into each participant: several had subsequently committed suicide, most of them had lost their ability to function normally. I have already spoken of the psychic/electric power we use to function: unfortunately, there are some very clever people who are able to tap into this power and harness other people's energy. This is what had happened to Gill.

One of the causes of Schizophrenia is, I believe, sensory overload. In Gill's case, the control mechanism had taken away her ability to selectively receive information, and she was hearing and receiving on all channels – rather like a radio picking up information on all wavelengths. Please be careful if you are given a crystal to take away with you from a workshop: there is the possibility that it could be used to contact your subconscious and steal energy.

Once I discovered that a crystal was being used with Gill, I could deal with the situation. It is possible, with practice, to travel beyond the pictures carried by an individual, and trace things through to the start of the problem. I realised that the energy from the people attending the course was being harnessed to a matrix, and this was providing energy for psychic experiments carried out by the organisers.

As before with Anne-the-crystal lady, I found myself standing in a room. In the centre of the room was a large matrix of metal (shaped like a hexagonal child's climbing frame). Electricity flashed about on this, and I noticed a large crystal nearby that was directing energy into it. Following the path away from the crystal, I could see many white energy lines leading to and from it. I realised that other course participants were also enmeshed. I am not subtle, as I have said before, and I threw a psychic tantrum because I was so angry. I released an enormous amount of psychic energy, directing it to the matrix. The metal matrix melted and the crystal that was directing energy into the matrix was also destroyed.

Gill was very vulnerable – for her own protection, I placed her in a greenhouse, so that she could no longer be used; I still had not found the crystal she had brought home with her from the course, so it was possible that a connection could be re-established through that. Within two weeks, Gill was out of the strait jacket completely, within three weeks she was home, and within two months she had stopped taking her drugs (not on my advice, I must stress). Two years down the line, I have released her gently from the greenhouse, and she is now functioning normally. The interesting thing about all this is that on a cognitive level she is unaware of my existence, or of the greenhouse. Her daughter and husband have begged me never to reveal to her how I helped.

The last bit

To lighten up this rather heavy final chapter, I am for fun going to talk about an incident that happened whilst I was talking to some young graduates, who were attending interviews for jobs.

Perhaps one of the more common 'phenomena' mentioned by emerging psychics is the party trick of guessing people's birthdays, their favourite colour, where they live. I am usually unable to do this... but on this occasion, I was, for some (obscure) reason, casually discussing psychic powers. I think it was probably because we had been talking about aerial photographs and I mentioned my dad. As I looked at their faces, I decided to try and distract them from worrying about the interviews by giving them some examples of psy ability. Looking at John, a tall serious man with a scholarly stoop and horn-rimmed glasses, I told him - off the top of my head - that he had been born on June 12th. I turned to Nigel, a rather intense Archaeological graduate, and told him that I might know that his granny lived in a house called Tivoli and that he had a goat called Martin.

Finally, I turned to Ruth, a red haired siren who subsequently touched many a male heart in our department. I gave as an example that her worst fear was to be buried alive in an Egyptian pyramid.

There was a complete silence. John cleared his throat... "Umm.... I was born on June 12th." Nigel tore his eyes away from my face, where they had been transfixed, and told me he did indeed have a goat called Martin and Tivoli was where his Gran lived. Ruth went as white as a sheet and nearly passed out.

There seems to be a block that prevents us directly accessing our psychic knowledge - I think it is either that too much power is applied or, more likely, that it requires lateral or sideways thinking: I thought I was only giving examples to the graduates, I didn't think I was going to be accurate!

I hope you have found this final chapter interesting and informative: It has been hard to find the right balance between too much background information, and too little. I hope you are now embarked serenely on your psychic travels. Good luck!

GLOSSARY OF UNUSED TERMS

(and in my humble opinion, unusable!)

Abandonment issue: Damn, I left my umbrella on the train again.

Chanelling: Using the remote control on your TV excessively.

Cutting the ties that bind: Letting out your clothes because you've put on weight

Empower: Plugging yourself into the ring main. NOT RECOMMENDED.

Energy cleansing: Getting down on your hands and knees to scrub the floor.

Higher consciousness: The feeling you get when you look over the edge on the 65th floor of a skyscraper.

Highest good: Usually this is one person's bid to justify imposing their will on everyone else.

Higher self: Absolutely no comment! (perhaps I haven't got one and I'm jealous).

Higher vibrations: I think this refers to a road drill in full flow.

Inner child: The spoilt bit of you that throws tantrums when you don't get your own way.

Inner self: The bit you hope no one ever sees, so you hide it behind technical and high-sounding words.

Mirroring: Going dinghy sailing (excuse the pun) or re-silvering the back of your favourite mirror.

Past life regression: Wallowing in the knowledge that your parents got it wrong sometimes, and therefore you have every right to behave appallingly to others.

Resonate: What all my victims did in the old days before I became better controlled.

Ribbons of Light: The ultimate in yuksville. Actually, I think it's a spiritual jellyfish swimming round on the astral plane and dangling its bits.

Soul mate: What you put on the bottom of your shoes so you don't slip.

Synchronicity: New-fashioned word for good, old-fashioned coincidence.

Transformation(al): Changing from a caterpillar into a sardine (or butterfly, whichever you prefer).

Universal love: Emasculated, de-sexed God.

The Universe: The benign place created by the emasculated de-sexed God, where presumably nothing ever goes wrong.

Appendix

KUNDALINI ENERGY

I'm going to throw one of the official explanations at you: if it means more to you than it does me, you're a lot clever than I am! Kundalini is the Sanskrit name given to the energy of primordial undifferentiated Absolute Consciousness, which, through evolution, has become limited in each living being. It is seen as a coiled serpent lying dormant inside the lowest chakra in the area of the base of the spine (yuk, I hate snakes) of all humans. Kundalini, once safely awakened in prepared individuals, expands the limited nature of human consciousness towards a totality of knowledge and experience that embraces the cosmos (not just the universe, note) and climaxes with the ultimate evolutionary consummation, termed Self-Realisation, or Union with God.

To be serious for a moment – I have met several people who are very seriously affected by a Kundalini experience; it has damaged both their physical and mental health. Please be careful – I don't understand myself what it is, but I do know it is extremely dangerous. My humble advice is steer clear!